THE WALK SERIES

THE WALK OF REPENTANCE

THE WALK
OF REPENTANCE

STEVE GALLAGHER

"Purity for Life"

www.purelifeministries.org

888.PURELIFE

EAN 978-0-9702202-8-8
ISBN 0-9702202-8-6

For other teaching materials from Pure Life Ministries
or copies of this book, contact:
Pure Life Ministries, 14 School Street, Dry Ridge, KY 41035
or call (888) 293-8714 or (859) 824-4444

www.purelifeministries.org
888.PURELIFE

THE WALK OF REPENTANCE

CONTENTS

INTRODUCTION

Welcome to the Pure Life Ministries study on *The Walk of Repentance,* a study about repentance: what it is, what kind of behavior and attitude we must repent of, and what it brings about—victory, abiding joy, and inner peace. But repentance isn't something you can just acquire information about and then go do it. *God* must bring repentance about in your heart.

The one thing most believers in America don't need more of is information *about* Christianity. We know more about it than any people who have ever lived. Our problem isn't a lack of knowledge; our problem is a lack of *living it.* This study has not been formulated to give a person more "head knowledge." The idea of it is to help the Word of God take root in your heart so that you can experience that true repentance.

As you go through the program, you will find that you will get out of it what you put into it. If you simply read it and quickly answer the questions, I'm afraid you will simply end up with more head knowledge. But if you will prayerfully take your time through each lesson, I know that God will do something wonderful in your life.

As you answer the questions, please feel free to expand your answers on another piece of paper (you might wish to keep a separate binder for your answers). Occasionally you will be asked to look a word up in a *Strong's Concordance.* If you don't own one, we would strongly urge you to get one. You will find it to be a tremendous tool in studying the Bible. But we would also encourage you—in addition to using the Strong's—to purchase a *Vine's Expository Dictionary.* You will find that it too is an invaluable tool in studying the meanings behind words. I should also mention that I use a New American Standard Bible. Occasionally you may need access to one.

The Lessons

Each week of this curriculum has a theme, with a different Bible study each day. For instance, Week Eleven is entitled, *Speaking Truth.* On Monday, you will study "delusion." On Tuesday, you will study "being truthful." On Wednesday, you will study "being deceitful." On Thursday, you will study "using flattery." And on Friday, you will study "gossip." All the studies combine to bring out realities about the need for truthfulness in our lives.

Each day you will have different types of studies. One day you may study one specific portion of Scripture, pulling out key truths from that section. Another day you may have to make a list of facts that are evident in another portion of Scripture. Still another day you may have to look up a word in the *Strong's* or *Vine's* and give the Greek or Hebrew meanings of the word. But one of the primary study methods you will be asked to use here will be to look up verses and write what you learn about that day's subject.

Let's say that the day's lesson is about "judgment." One of the verses you are asked to look up is I Corinthians 3:12-13. It says:

> "Now if any man builds upon the foundation with gold, silver, precious stones, wood, hay, straw, each man's work will become evident; for the day will show it, because it is to be revealed with fire; and the fire itself will test the quality of each man's work."

Your assignment is to read the passage and tell what you learn about it. The answer many would give to this verse would be something like this:

> "We will be judged by the kind of work we do. That which is good—gold, silver, & precious stones will remain and we will get a reward for it. That which wasn't good—wood, hay & straw—will be burned up. The fire of the Holy Spirit will burn away the work that isn't done with the right heart and will show what it was really made of."

What you have here is a sort of commentary on what the verse says. In essence, the person has just rewritten the passage; sort of summed up the meaning of it. It is apparent that he hasn't prayed over the Scripture and sought God about its meaning *for his life*. The answer he has given is somewhat shallow. When you do the studies, spend a few minutes in prayer before you study it. Ask God to show you what He wants you to get out of it. Remember one thing: *He has something special for you everyday in His Word!* Come to expect it!

After praying about it, chew on the words for a few minutes. "If any man builds....builds.... what does building have to do with my judgment? What am I building? OK, I see from the previous verse that the foundation for this building is Jesus Christ, but what am I building? Oh! What about that passage in Matthew 7 where Jesus tells about the man who built his house on the rock and the one who built his house on sand? Let me look that up real quick and see what He shows me there...."

"OK, I can see that I am building my life on this foundation, and that I will be judged by how my life has lined up *with the will of God*. What else can I learn here about my own life? Let's see... What is the difference between gold, silver, precious stones and wood, hay and straw? Well, the first group are lasting. They are valuable. They don't burn. They are beautiful to look upon. Maybe the Lord is showing me that when I am obeying His will my life looks beautiful! Maybe when it is really built on the foundation of Christ, my life will truly touch others and the effects will last an eternity.

"What else? Each man's work....My work.... What *is* my work? What has God called me to do in life? Well, I know that my work is to love others and to live a life of mercy to others. I know that I can look spiritual to others, but one day I will stand before the Lord and all my self-serving motives will be revealed. Okay, let me put down my answer:"

"This passage of Scripture shows me that if I build my house upon the foundation of Christ, if I live my life in accordance with His will—as shown in the story of Matthew 7—then my life will appear as beautiful as gold, silver, & precious stones when the Lord looks upon it. I will be rewarded with eternal treasures. But when I do things *my* way, then my efforts will be burned up! I know that I will be judged—not on how spiritual I may appear to others—but on how much love I have really shown to others. The truth about my life and motives will be revealed when I stand before the Lord."

Can you now see the difference between someone who prayerfully put his heart into the question, and someone who just scribbled out the first thing that came to his mind? The answer given here isn't that much longer, it's just more personal, more relevant and effective. The more prayer and effort you put into these studies, the more you will find your heart changing!

Christian Stories

At the end of each week you will find the story of the Church woven in character studies of different Christians down through the centuries. The purpose for this is simple. It is my hope that, as you read these stories, you will be deeply affected by the level of devotion of others who have served God. Their relationship with the Lord was all they had, and it showed by their lives. As you go through these stories, please ask God to show you what Christianity is really all about.

Well, you're all set! Get started this coming Monday and stay faithful everyday. God will use it to help *you* find the deep, heart-felt walk of repentance I know you desire.

WEEK 1: BIBLICAL SUBMISSION

Monday   TRUE ACCOUNTABILITY

MEMORY VERSE: HEBREWS 13:17

With the advent of so many support groups in America today, "accountability" has become one of the big "buzz words" of our culture. Those of us who have struggled with life-dominating habits have learned to meet together so that we can be answerable to each other about how we are doing with that problem. But the principle of *accountability* in the Bible means much more than just telling another person how we have done with our particular problem that week. It means that we should hold our entire lives accountable to those believers we have joined ourselves with. It is one of the tremendous tools the Lord has given us in our own personal war with sin.

Unfortunately, however, because of our mobile society and the make-up of our large churches, believers find it very easy to attend church without any true accountability. This is one of the great tragedies of the American Church today: millions of Christians "doing their own thing," without being answerable to the leadership God has placed over them and even to each other. This is one of the main reasons sin is so rampant today in our churches.

1. Write out Ephesians 5:21 and explain what you think it means.

2. Read Acts 4:32-5:16. Explain how the selfless acts of generosity of the early Christians contributed to an atmosphere of mutual support in the Church. Please take your time, think this question through, and make your answer thorough.

1. Look up the following verses on submission and subjection. Write out what you have learned about these principles in the space provided.

   a. Luke 2:51

   b. Romans 13:5

   c. I Corinthians 16:15-16

   d. Ephesians 5:24

   e. I Peter 5:5

2. Now look up the word "submit" in the back of your *Strong's Concordance*. The same Greek word (#5293) is used in each of the above instances. Write out the Greek word and its English definition.

The opposite of submission is rebellion. Rebellion comes from a stubborn independence and a prideful attitude that a person should not have to accept authority. When Christ was asked to submit to the authority of God's will, He said "…not My will but Thine." When Satan was asked to submit, he refused.

1. Read the passage about Satan's downfall in Isaiah 14:12-15. Write out Satan's five "I wills." and the final outcome of his actions.

    1.

    2.

    3.

    4.

    5.

    Outcome:

2. Now read the passage about Christ's exaltation in Philippians 2:5-11. Write out five of the steps Jesus took in submission to the Father. Write out His final outcome.

    1.

    2.

    3.

    4.

    5.

    Outcome:

3. Can you see the opposite paths taken and the outcome of each? Write out Matthew 23:12.

1. Write out Hebrews 13:17 and what this verse means to your life, especially in your present situation.

2. Richard Wurmbrand, a Romanian pastor who spent fourteen years being tortured in communist prisons (see Week 23) said the following about spiritual authority:

> "I can admit of no independent free-lances in Christianity. Christians are soldiers who belong to an army. They have commanders, and must obey them. Christ himself "gave some apostles… some pastors and teachers". Nobody can be a Christian and declare Jesus as his only pastor, just as nobody can obey a general while refusing obedience to the captain, or even the sergeant, though these may be less competent than the commander-in-chief.
>
> "We used to live under a free enterprise system, and we have applied to our churches principles and ideas taken from this system. But Christianity is not of this world. There is no such thing as free enterprise in Christianity. There is organization, hierarchy and, I repeat, obedience."[1]

Can you see any "free enterprise" attitudes in your heart in regard to Christianity? Do you tend to see yourself as being independent of the leadership of others? Explain your answers.

3. At this present stage of your Christian life, what position in God's army would you consider yourself to be in (general, sergeant, private, etc.)? Explain why you see yourself in that position.

The thing we must understand about biblical submission is that we are not called to be in submission to the man, but to the *position of authority* God has placed him in. It is this same case with police officers. We obey that man because he has a badge on his chest which is the emblem of the authority that has been vested in him by our government. Although we are a free nation with individual rights, we don't have the right to disobey a police officer when he is acting on behalf of the government.

In I Peter 2:18-23, we find the apostle talking to slaves about being submitted to their masters. But even though we aren't slaves, some valuable insights are given in this section of Scripture regarding submission to leadership. Read these verses and answer the following questions:

1. What kind of leaders (masters) should we submit to? (verse 18)

2. What finds favor with God? (verses 19-20)

3. What example did Christ leave us to follow? (verses 21-24)

4. By responding to evil men the way He did, who did He entrust His situation to? (verse 23)

Read the following verses about Jesus Christ, and describe what He went through for our sake.

1. Philippians 2:5-7

2. Isaiah 53:3

3. John 6:66

4. Psalm 22:6-8

5. John 7:5

6. Matthew 26:67-68

7. Mark 15:16-20

8. John 19:17-18

9. Psalm 22:14-18

WEEK 2: THE CONFRONTIVE NATURE

Monday   GOD'S DEALINGS WITH MAN

MEMORY VERSE: PROVERBS 3:11-12

Since the garden of Eden, God has had to deal with the rebellion of His people. Look up the following verses and tell how God deals with it.

1. Genesis 3:17-19

2. Exodus 32:9-10

3. II Samuel 12:7-12

4. Jeremiah 23:1-2

5. Matthew 3:7-10

6. Matthew 23:13

1. Write out II Timothy 3:16-17.

2. What are the four things that the Word of God is profitable for?

    1.

    2.

    3.

    4.

3. Write out what *you* think each word means and then look up each word in the Vine's Dictionary and see what else you can learn about it.

    1.

    2.

    3.

    4.

4. And finally, according to the verse, what is the purpose for these four things?

Read the following verses and explain the meaning of each in your own words.

1. Proverbs 9:7-8

2. Proverbs 12:1,15

3. Proverbs 10:17

4. Proverbs 15:12

5. Proverbs 17:10

6. Proverbs 29:1

7. Proverbs 15:31-32

1. In yesterday's study we found the importance of accepting godly reproof with maturity and wisdom. Today we want to learn about having a teachable spirit as a child. Read the following verses and write what you learn about children.

    a. Matthew 19:14

    b. Matthew 18:3

    c. Matthew 18:4

    d. Matthew 11:25-26

    e. Psalms 103:13

2. What do you think makes children generally have such a teachable spirit?

In the first letter Paul wrote to the Corinthian church, he confronted them about many different things in the church that weren't right; i.e. sexual sin, strife, greed, etc. Let us now read the outcome of that confrontation (and hopefully the outcome of *all* biblical confrontation). Read II Corinthians 7:6-16 and answer the following questions.

1. In verse 7, write out the three words that describe the new attitude of the Corinthians after accepting reproof.

    1.

    2.

    3.

2. Go through this portion of Scripture and count the number of times Paul uses the words "sorry," "sorrow" or "sorrowful."

3. According to verses 9 and 10, what does *godly* sorrow over sin bring about?

4. What does *worldly* sorrow bring about?

5. Godly sorrow is the mourning one goes through when he has grieved the Spirit of God with sin. When you are only sorry about your sin because you got caught or because of its consequences, what kind of sorrow would you call it?

6. According to verse 10, what is the ultimate end of only having this latter kind of sorrow?

1. Read Philippians 3:4-8 and describe what Paul gave up to become a follower of Christ.

2. Read II Corinthians 4:8-10 and try to describe what it was like for Paul to carry the weight of bringing the gospel to the Gentiles.

3. Read II Corinthians 6:4-5 and list the ten types of suffering Paul endured to bring the gospel to the Gentiles.

   1.   6.

   2.   7.

   3.   8.

   4.   9.

   5.   10.

WEEK 3: THE REPENTANT HEART

Monday   THE PREACHING OF JOHN AND JESUS

MEMORY VERSE: ACTS 3:19

1. Look up the following verses and write out what was said by John or Jesus.

   a. Matthew 3:2

   b. Matthew 3:8

   c. Mark 1:15

   d. Matthew 4:17

2. If Jesus were to come to American churches today, what do you think the first thing would be that He would preach?

3. Look up "repent" in the *Strong's Concordance* and in the *Vine's Dictionary* and give the definition.

The Sermon on the Mount was probably the first sermon Jesus preached at length. In it, He gives the elements and characteristics of true repentance.

1. Write out Matthew 5:3.

2. Read Luke 18:9-14

 a. According to verse 9, who did Jesus tell this parable to?

 b. According to verse 9, what is the outcome of a self-righteous attitude?

 c. According to verse 11, who was the Pharisee concerned mostly with?

 d. According to verse 11, whose appearance was the Pharisee concerned mostly about?

 e. According to verse 11, what things did he say to make himself look good?

 f. According to verse 12, what things did he say to make himself look good?

 g. According to verse 14, did his attitude bring justification from sin before God?

3. How often do you—whether in your mind or out loud to others—attempt to make yourself look good by puffing yourself up or by putting others down?

   a. List the ways that you puff yourself up.

   b. List the ways you put others down to make yourself look good.

Read Luke 18:9-14 again and answer the following questions.

1. In verse 13, Jesus said the tax-gatherer was unwilling to even stand close to the Pharisee. Would you say it was because he thought he was more spiritual than the Pharisee?

2. In verse 13, Jesus quoted the tax-gatherer as saying, "God be merciful to me, *the* sinner!" Do you think that this tax-gatherer had any concern about *the Pharisee's* sinfulness?

3. Do you think it would be safe to say that he was blinded to the sins of others because he was so broken over his own sin?

4. Would you say that this describes the attitude of your heart?

5. If not, describe what you think you need to do to gain this attitude. Take your time and answer this question prayerfully.

Read Luke 18:9-14.

1. In verse 13, Jesus said this publican (tax-gatherer) was unwilling to even look up to heaven. E.M. Bounds, one of the greatest prayer warriors in the history of the Church, once wrote, "We should go to God's throne as a beggar at the door of a rich man." However, in the Church today there are many leaders who seem to teach that we should go to God with a demanding, arrogant attitude. They often use Hebrews 4:15-16 as their text. But I believe they take this verse out of context. Read Hebrews 4:15-16 and describe what you think the writer was talking about when he said we should come boldly to the throne of grace.

2. Read James 4:3 and write down what you learn about prayer.

3. Read I John 5:14-15 and explain whose will we should be concerned with when we approach God's throne.

4. Have you ever used prayer as a way to try to get God to do what *you* thought He should do in your life? Explain how:

1. Write out Matthew 5:4.

2. Read Luke 7:36-50 and answer the following questions.

   a. Have you ever put pressure on yourself to look your best to spiritual leaders? Tell about it.

   b. Can you see the brokenness in this woman's heart about her sinful condition?

   c. Can you see the lack of brokenness in the hearts of the Pharisees?

   d. Can you see the judgmental attitude that they held in regard to her sin?

3. Looking over your own general spiritual condition, would you say your heart tends to be more like this woman's, or the Pharisees'? Explain your answer.

It began with Stephen, stoned to death after a forceful sermon. Next, James the brother of John was beheaded. Then every other disciple except John was martyred. Since that time, millions upon millions have been put to death for claiming the name of Christ. For us who live in a time of peace and prosperity, it is often hard to imagine having to pay a price for our Christianity. What is so startling isn't so much that Christians have been persecuted and martyred for their faith, but that so many have done so in such a joyful manner.

The following are but two of many stories of those who, faced with a choice of life without Christ or horrible death, joyfully chose the latter.

The Apostle Andrew, according to the early writer Jerome, went about preaching Christ all across the Roman empire. While in Achaia, he was called in by Aegeas, the governor of the region, to answer for his actions before a council of officials. He was accused by the council of attempting to persuade men to join the outlawed "sect" called Christians. Andrew readily admitted to this and went on to say that the deities the Romans worshiped were nothing more than devils.

The proconsul, infuriated by Andrew's comments, warned him that if he continued to preach such things he would soon be fastened to a cross with all speed. According to Jerome, Andrew replied, "I would not have preached the honor and glory of the cross, if I feared the death of the cross." Aegeas immediately sentenced him to be crucified.

Andrew, going to the place of crucifixion, didn't shrink back nor show any fear. But out of his heart came the following exultation: "O cross, most welcome and long looked for! With a willing mind, joyfully and desirously, I come to thee, being the scholar of Him which did hang on thee: because I have always been thy lover, and have coveted to embrace thee."

It was in the second century that the beloved Polycarp, the bishop of Smyrna, lived. A hot persecution broke out at that time against the church in Smyrna, bringing to death many brave Christians.

But it was Polycarp who the persecutors desired most. They searched and searched for him and finally found him late one evening. He could have escaped but refused, simply saying, "The will of the Lord be done." Hearing that the soldiers had come for him, he came out with a cheerful countenance and immediately ordered food to be brought for all of the men. They were amazed by the old man's calm composure and agreed with his request to allow him to spend an hour in prayer before departing.

He was then taken to see the proconsul of the region. At first the proconsul attempted to persuade Polycarp to denounce Christ by appealing to his age. When this proved futile, he attempted to threaten him into compliance. Polycarp answered him, "Eighty-six years have I served Him, and He has never done me any harm. How could I blaspheme my King and Savior?"

The proconsul threatened to let him be ripped asunder by wild beasts. Polycarp calmly replied, "Let them come." The proconsul then threatened to have him burned to death, whereupon Polycarp replied, "You threaten me with a fire that burns but for an hour and goes out after a short time, for you do not know the fire of the coming judgment and of the eternal punishment for the godless. Why do you wait? Bring on whatever you will."

It is said that while he spoke to the proconsul his face shone with an inward light, and he was not the least bit disconcerted with the man's threats. He was then taken out to a stake while wood was piled around him. When the executioner attempted to nail him to the stake, he simply said, "Let me be. He who gives me the strength to endure the fire will also give me the strength to remain at the stake unflinching, without the security of your nails."

The story of Polycarp's calmness in the face of death spread quickly across the Church. His courage proved to be a source of courage for many others as well.

WEEK 4 : THE FRUIT OF REPENTANCE

Monday   THE PRAYER OF REPENTANCE

MEMORY VERSE: PSALM 51:1

Poverty of spirit is a condition of the heart whereby a person sees their total need of a Savior. Out of that attitude comes a brokenness and a sorrow over one's sin. How seldom this is seen in America, though. Richard Wurmbrand once said, "I hear a whole lot of laughing in America but very little weeping..." He was referring to our lack of concern over our own sin and the sin in the lives of others who are on their way to an eternity in hell.

1. Read Matthew 5:3-4. Take a moment and ask God to give you the attitude Jesus spoke of.

2. Read Psalm 51 and answer the following questions.

   a. Can you see any correlation between David's first few words and the words of the tax-gatherer in Luke 18?

   b. According to verse 1, did David entreat God's grace according to his own righteousness, or according to God's compassion?

   c. What kind of picture comes into your mind from reading verse 2?

   d. According to verse 3, how often was David thinking of his sin?

   e. According to verse 4, would you say that David was accepting responsibility for his actions?

   f. According to verse 5, would you agree that David saw his sinful condition from birth?

   g. According to verse 6, what must we be in order to receive God's wisdom?

1. Write out the following verses and what you learn in each of them.

   a. Psalm 34:18

   b. Psalm 51:17

   c. Isaiah 57:15

   d. Isaiah 66:2

2. Explain what you think "contrition" is, and any experiences that you have had with this attitude.

Meekness has been compared to a stallion who has been broken by his master. Before he was broken, he was independent and thereby useless to his master. Once broken, he could be controlled, guided and used.

1. Read the following verses and tell what you learn of meekness from them.

    a. Matthew 5:5

    b. Ephesians 4:1-2

    c. Psalm 25:9

    d. Psalm 76:8-9

    e. II Timothy 2:24-25

2. Explain what areas of your life exhibit self-determination, self-sufficiency, and pride (rather than meekness).

1. Write out Matthew 5:6.

2. Author Kay Arthur compares this to a starving man in the desert, who desperately needs food and water. Do you feel *desperation* or *contentment* about your spiritual condition?

3. Write out Matthew 5:7.

4. Look up the following verses and tell what you have learned about mercy.

   a. Micah 6:8

   b. Matthew 9:13

   c. James 2:13

5. Look up Luke 6:36 and briefly tell what God has done in your life, to make it possible for you to be merciful to others.

1. Write out Matthew 5:8.

2. While this verse could have to do with purity from sin, it very likely may refer more to sincerity of *motives*. When we are broken by God over the sinfulness of our hearts, it begins a cleansing process of *what motivates us* to love and serve Him. We often begin to detect motives in our hearts that are more self-serving than they are concerned with pleasing God. If you can think of any motives in your heart about why you live the Christian life that you don't think are right, list them now.

3. Write out Matthew 5:9.

4. Write out Proverbs 16:7.

5. Explain how a contrite spirit would bring peace into a situation.

The following is part of a letter written by Christians who lived in France in the year 177.

"The servants of Christ who live as aliens at Vienne and Lyons in Gaul, to the brothers in Asia Minor and Phrygia... The Adversary has fallen upon us with all his might. He has given us a foretaste of the ignominy of his future when it breaks in ....

"Matures, Sanctus, Blandina, and Attalus were taken to the wild beasts in the amphitheater, to give the pagan crowd which was gathered there a public spectacle of inhumanity. They ran the gauntlet of whips. They were already used to this. They let themselves be dragged around and mauled by the wild beasts. Everything the raving, yelling mob wanted, now from this side, now from that, they endured. They sat upon the iron chair which roasted their bodies so that the fumes rose up. Yet they heard nothing from Sanctus beyond the confession of faith he had repeated over and over again from the beginning. When they were still found alive in spite of the terrible and prolonged torture, they were finally killed. Blandina was hung on a post, delivered up to the wild beasts for food. Hung up like this in the shape of the Cross, she could be seen from afar, and through her ardent prayers she aroused increased zeal in those who were fighting... As none of the wild beasts had yet touched Blandina, she was taken down from the post and thrown into prison once more, to be kept ready for a new fight...

"The glorified Blandina had already learned to know the scourging, the wild beasts, and the red-hot griddle. Finally they tied her in a fishing net and threw her to a bull. For a long time the animal tossed her about, and so she was killed."[2]

Foxe's Book of Martyrs tells the following story about this servant girl who willingly suffered so much for her faith in Christ.

"(Blandina) dreaded that she would not be able to witness a good confession, because of the weakness of her body. Blandina was endued with so much fortitude, that those who successively tortured her from morning to night were quite worn out with fatigue, owned themselves conquered and exhausted of their whole apparatus of tortures, and were amazed to see her still breathing whilst her body was torn and laid open. The blessed woman recovered fresh vigor in the act of confession; and it was an evident annihilation of all her pains, to say—"I am a Christian, and no evil is committed among us ....

"The blessed Blandina, last of all... hastened to undergo (sufferings) herself, rejoicing and triumphing in her exit, as if invited to a marriage supper, not as one going to be exposed to wild beasts. After she had endured stripes, the tearing of the beasts, and the iron chair, she was enclosed in a net, and thrown to a bull; and having been tossed some time by the animal, and proving quite superior to her pains, through the influence of hope... at length breathed out her soul."[3]

WEEK 5: THE LIFESTYLE AND ATTITUDE OF REPENTANCE

Monday   FALSE TEACHERS

MEMORY VERSE: MATTHEW 7:21

1. Read Matthew 7:15-20 and answer the following questions.

   a. According to verse 15, who do the false prophets look like?

   b. According to verse 16, how will you know who they are?

2. Look up the following verses and write what you have learned about the lives and ministries of false teachers.

   a. Jeremiah 23:16-17

   b. Romans 16:17-18

   c. II Corinthians 2:17

   d. Philippians 1:15-17

   e. II Timothy 4:3

1. Read Matthew 7:21-23 and answer the following questions.

    a. There are many who align themselves with evangelical Christianity by the church they go to, the radio shows they listen to, the books they read. But according to verse 21, who will be those who enter the kingdom of heaven?

    b. According to verse 22, what are the works of some of those who claim to be followers of Christ but are destined for hell?

    c. According to verse 23, did Jesus ever really have a true relationship with these people?

2. Read Matthew 13:3-23 and answer the following questions.

    a. According to verse 19, why weren't these saved?

    b. According to verses 20 and 21, why weren't these saved?

    c. According to verse 22, why weren't these saved?

    d. According to verse 23, what is the sign of those who are saved?

3. Look up the word "fruit" in the *Strong's Concordance* and the *Vine's Dictionary*. Explain what you think Jesus meant by this term.

1. Write out Matthew 5:20.

2. Write out James 2:10 and explain why you are saved but the Pharisees were not.

3. Read Matthew 6:1-18 and list the four things the Lord warns us not to do to be seen by men.

    1.

    2.

    3.

    4.

4. Explain why you think it is important not to do these before men.

5. List the ways you practice your good deeds before others.

Read Matthew 5:21-48. For each of the following sections of Scripture, tell the law that is quoted from the Old Testament, and then write the attitude we should have regarding that law.

1. Matthew 5:21-26

2. Matthew 5:27-30

3. Matthew 5:31-32

4. Matthew 5:33-37

5. Matthew 5:38-42

6. Matthew 5:43-48

Read Matthew 5:10-16 and answer the following questions.

1. According to verse 10, why are they persecuted?

2. In last week's study we found that the person who lived a life of brokenness would bring peace with others. And yet Jesus said, "I did not come to bring peace, but a sword." Jesus wasn't persecuted because of His gentleness and humility, but because He testified of the darkness and sin in the world. According to verse 11, what three things can we expect when we truly live for Christ?

     1.

     2.

     3.

3. According to verse 12, what do you have to gain by being persecuted for the sake of Christ?

4. According to verse 13, what happens to ineffective salt?

5. According to verses 14-16, what should we do with our Christian witness?

6. According to verse 16, what other outcome besides persecution can we expect when we live repentant lives before others?

For almost three hundred years, to be a Christian meant persecution, suffering and often death. This all changed in the year 312 when Emperor Constantine accepted Christianity as a legitimate religion in the Roman empire. During the fourth century, Christianity went from being a small, persecuted sect to being the official religion of the empire.

Although this was a major victory for Christianity at the time (comparable to the collapse of communism for Russian Christians), in the long run it proved to come at great cost. With the rise of religious freedom came many cultic teachings. Heresy abounded everywhere. But even worse than that was that suddenly being a bishop in the Church changed from being a position that usually ended in the mouth of a lion in the Coliseum, to being a position of tremendous influence in the empire. The gradual outcome of this was that soon, rather than the godly and meek rising to leadership, those who were filled with self-ambition fought their way to the top.

From the time of Paul's imprisonment, the church that met in Rome gradually became the most vibrant and important of the churches around the empire. This became all the more so when Constantine officially ended all persecution of Christianity. Suddenly being the bishop of the church in Rome became a very important position to have. The man holding this position eventually became known as the pope.

Another detrimental effect that Constantine had on the Christian Church were the pagan ideas he helped see integrated into the Church. Constantine had always believed in the worship of many gods. His favorite god was the Unconquered Sun. Although many believe he became a bona-fide Christian, whether he did or not, it is still clear that he brought many of his old practices into the Church. The first day of the week became a holiday known as "the venerable day of the Sun." The birthday of the Sun, December 25, became the day Christ's birth was celebrated. *Saturnalia*, the Roman winter festival also celebrated around this time of the year, provided the merriment, gift-giving and candles typical of later Christmas holidays. The veneration of the Virgin Mary was also probably stimulated by other pagan religions. The idea of there being a "mother of heaven" goes back to the worship of the Phoenician goddess Ashtar (who had a baby son and yet was known as "the Great Virgin"). Easter (from Ashtar) became the holiday to celebrate Christ's death.

So, although at the time that the terrible persecution stopped there must have been a tremendous shout of joy heard in heaven, our Heavenly Father knew how it would hurt real Christianity. For the first three hundred years of its existence, Christianity was marked by red-hot persecution and red-hot fervency. As the persecution stopped, the fervency for God waned.

Over the next twelve hundred years, all the way to the Reformation, to be a Christian meant to follow the path laid out by the Catholic Church. Gradually, more and more unbiblical practices were added to Catholicism. The pope gradually came to be viewed as God's official spokesman to the world; thereby even giving his words the weight of Scripture.

During these "dark ages," lay people were not allowed to read the Bible. The only versions to be found were written in Latin so that only Catholic priests could read them. If people wanted to know of God, they could only learn what the priests taught them. Those who dared to question the system often found themselves in the hands of the "inquisition." The inquisitors had complete authority to act as prosecutor, judge and jury. People in their hands often spent years languishing in medieval prisons of torture. All of this began to set the stage for the coming Reformation.

WEEK 6: THE PROCESS OF REPENTANCE

Monday   CHANGE TAKES TIME

MEMORY VERSE: JAMES 1:21-22

God is ever in the business of changing His people into the image of Christ. He does this through experiences, through gradual changes in our hearts, through stages of spiritual drought and through times of great victory. In one area of life He might do a slow, gradual work of changing us. In another area of life He may leave us at a plateau for several years and then suddenly use one experience to bring about great repentance and change. It all works together in His wonderful plan to mold us into vessels of use.

Look up the following verses and tell what you learn in each of them about what God is doing in your life.

1. Philippians 1:6

2. Philippians 2:13

3. II Corinthians 4:16

4. Romans 8:28-29

5. Isaiah 64:8

When a person is confronted with sin in his life—whether in person by a loved one, by a message from the pulpit, or even just by reading the Word—he is faced with making a decision about this information. James said, "But prove yourselves to be doers of the Word, not merely hearers who delude themselves." When you "hear" the Word, you must decide what you will do with it. Either you will repent of your sin or you will go into delusion. The following are five ways that people side-step repentance.

1. *Blameshifting* – When a person doesn't want to accept the truth about his sinful behavior, he will often attempt to shift the blame onto someone else to get the focus off his own actions. Read the story of Adam and Eve in Genesis 3:6-13. Tell how you see blameshifting at work here.

2. *Delayed Repentance* – Another thing people do is to admit they have a problem but to delay dealing with it. "I'm not ready to deal with this issue yet," is often said. But the Psalmist wrote, "I hastened and did not delay to keep Thy commandments." Read the following two verses where Paul had preached to unbelievers and write out their responses.

    1. Acts 17:32

    2. Acts 24:25

3. *Self-Justification* – When confronted with sin, people also attempt to justify their actions or behavior. King Saul did this when he offered a sacrifice to the Lord instead of waiting for Samuel as he had been told to do. Read I Samuel 13:11-12 and tell of Saul's excuse for his disobedience.

4. *Minimizing* – Another thing we often do when confronted is to discount the wrongness of our actions. Read I Samuel 15:19-20 and tell what Saul said to minimize his wrong-doing.

5. *Attack* – And lastly, as we have already seen in an earlier lesson, people often attack the messenger God sends to confront their sin. Read Proverbs 9:7-8 and list the three things that a person can expect when he attempts to reprove an unrepentant person in sin.

    1.

    2.

    3.

The whole idea behind repentance is to change from a sinful lifestyle to one lived out in obedience to God. We have gotten in the "habit" of living our lives in accordance to the desires of the flesh and the practices of the world. We must now change those old, bad habits and learn to be in the "habit" of doing things God's way.

1. Read Colossians 3:1-17. List ten old habits that should be done away with and ten new habits that should be acquired.

   Old   New

   1.   1.

   2.   2.

   3.   3.

   4.   4.

   5.   5.

   6.   6.

   7.   7.

   8.   8.

   9.   9.

   10.   10.

2. What bad habits from this list have you already overcome?

3. What good habits from this list have you already acquired or are working on?

There is a principle found in the Bible which Paul coined: "putting off and putting on." Look up the following verses, and tell for each one what should be put off or put on.

1. Ephesians 4:22

2. Ephesians 4:24

3. Ephesians 4:25

4. Colossians 3:8

5. Colossians 3:9

6. Colossians 3:10

7. Colossians 3:14

1. Read James 1:21-25 and answer the following questions.

   a. According to verse 21, what is about to save our souls?

   b. And with what kind of attitude should we receive it?

   c. If a person receives the Word with an attitude that he already "knows it all," according to verse 22, what do you think will happen to him?

   d. According to verses 23 and 24, what happens to the person who hears the Word but doesn't act upon it?

   e. How significant do you think James's illustration of the mirror is for this portion of Scripture?

   f. What does James say the person forgets when he walks away from the mirror?

   g. According to verse 25, what does James say the man is who is a doer of the Word?

2. Read Matthew 7:24-27 and explain how this story relates to the teaching in James.

Many things contributed to the coming about of the Reformation. Across Europe, seeds of change were taking root in the different people groups. The fifteenth and sixteenth centuries were a time of great social upheaval. Explorers were traveling all over the world on behalf of the leading European nations. Interest in the arts, philosophy and science were renewed. In general, people were breaking out of the closed society that had typified life during the Dark Ages.

And it was in this time of great opportunity that God raised up special men to lead people to know Him in a way that wasn't possible before. There were several men who paved the way for the great reformers of the sixteenth century. John Wycliffe, who lived in the fourteenth century, tried himself to bring about reformation; but it just wasn't time yet. His teachings did pave the way for others, however.

One of Wycliffe's chief beneficiaries was Jan Hus, who was ordained as a priest in 1401. In his teachings he stressed the need for personal piety and purity of life. He also taught that only the Word of God could establish doctrine and that neither popes nor cardinals had this right. He fought against the worshipping of images, belief in false miracles and the selling of indulgences. In 1415 Hus attended the Council of Constance to defend his beliefs. Although his safety had been guaranteed by the Emperor, he was tried as a heretic and burned at the stake.

The Reformation began on the eve of All Souls day on October 31, 1517. On that day Martin Luther, a professor of biblical studies at an obscure university in Germany posted what has become known as *95 Theses*. It was common in those days for priests or teachers to post teachings or notices in a public place. The young monk simply wrote his concerns about the abuses in the Church in the sale of indulgences.

The people were taught during this time that if they had been forgiven and blessed by a priest before death, that they would then enter a place called Purgatory. The Church taught that before the person could enter heaven, he had to spend an indeterminate amount of time in Purgatory to be cleansed of the sins he had committed in life. If the person bought an indulgence from the Church, he could earn time off in Purgatory. It was nothing more than a papal scheme to raise money for the building of great cathedrals in Rome.

Nobody could have envisioned what would come about from this obscure monk's notice. Within a few days, every university and religious center in Europe knew about it. At first, the pope didn't take the matter seriously. But Martin Luther found himself being swept away in a movement he had no intention of beginning. Within three years he was excommunicated by the pope and the following year, outlawed by the Emperor.

The people were ready for a leader such as Luther. They were clamoring for reform; having grown weary of the many abuses and errors of the Catholic Church. Martin Luther became one of the most controversial men who have ever lived. There seemed to be no middle ground as his teachings split Europe.

But while he sheepishly enjoyed the popularity of his followers, he withstood tremendous opposition from his peers within the Church. It is no easy thing to stand up against one's peers, especially when one stands entirely alone. Martin Luther was a very brave man who continually found himself on his face before God, pleading for the strength to endure the incredible resistance he continually encountered.

Nevertheless, he refused to back down. For twenty-five years he wrote about the abuses of the Catholic Church and the necessity to come to God by faith alone. While his teachings were not that much different from some of the other reformers, his timing on the scene was perfect. Through his faithful obedience to his Savior, Martin Luther was used in a powerful way to change the entire history of God's dealings with man.

WEEK 7: OVERCOMING SELF

Monday   SELFISHNESS

MEMORY VERSE: PHILIPPIANS 2:3-4

1. Write out Matthew 7:12.

2. Look up the following verses and write what you have learned about selfishness.

   a. Isaiah 5:8

   b. I John 3:17

   c. Matthew 25:31-46

   d. James 2:15-16

3. Living a selfish lifestyle keeps a sexual addict in the habit of living life in the pursuit of his own self-centered desires. Explain how you see the selfishness of your own life contributing to your habits of sexual sin.

UNSELFISHNESS

Read the following verses and tell how the person was being unselfish.

1. Genesis 13:9

2. Genesis 50:21

3. Numbers 11:29

4. I Samuel 18:4

5. Daniel 5:17

6. I Corinthians 10:33

7. II Corinthians 8:9

1. Look up the following verses and write them out.

    a. Philippians 2:4

    b. Romans 15:1

    c. I Corinthians 10:24

2. Read Luke 6:30-37 and write out in your own words the kind of lifestyle we should lead as Christians.

3. According to Luke 6:38, how can we expect our Heavenly Father to treat us when we treat others this way?

1. Read the following verses and tell what you learn about following Christ.

 a. Mark 10:28-31

 b. Luke 14:16-24

 c. Luke 14:26-27

 d. Luke 14:28-33

 e. Philippians 3:7-8

2. What have you refused to forsake for your Savior?

Look up the following verses and tell what you learn about self control.

1. Proverbs 17:27

2. Proverbs 25:16

3. Proverbs 25:28

4. Proverbs 27:7

5. Galatians 5:22-23

6. II Corinthians 10:4-5

7. II Timothy 1:7

About the same time Martin Luther's actions were shaking Europe, an Englishman named William Tyndale quietly began translating the Bible into English. Tyndale had a burning desire to see Scriptures in the hands of laypeople. Once he commented to a priest, "If God spare my life, ere many years pass I will cause a boy that driveth the plough shall know more of the Scriptures than thou doest."

He set about the task by enlisting the financial support of merchants in London. William worked tirelessly on the project but in 1535, while in Brussels, he was strangled to death and burned. Nevertheless, before his death he had managed to translate the entire New Testament and part of the Old Testament into English. Several more translations came out during the next century, culminating in the King James Version which was published in 1611. Much of this version was taken from the work of Tyndale.

Another of the great Reformers of this period was a young Frenchman named John Calvin. While attending the University of Paris he came upon the teachings of Luther. It was about this time that he experienced a sudden conversion. He later said, "God subdued and brought my heart to docility. It was more hardened against such matters than was to be expected in such a young man."

After this, he broke with the Catholic Church and lived in exile in Basle. While there he began to formulate his theology which came out in his first edition of *The Institutes of the Christian Religion*. Later he came to Geneva and managed to set up a Christian led government in the city. He attempted to bring every citizen under the moral discipline of the church, but met with much resistance. At one time, even one of his critics was arrested and burned alive. Nevertheless, Calvin's contributions to our understanding of Christianity were great. His main focus of teaching was on the sovereignty of God; that before the foundation of the earth God chose some for salvation and some for destruction. Although he too was fiercely opposed, he lived until illness took his life at the age of fifty-five.

While Luther led the spiritual revolt in Germany and Calvin did in Geneva, a man named Huldreich Zwingli led the movement in Zurich. Zwingli was a contemporary of Luther, but would not go as far in his teachings. He worked with the city council of Zurich, combining church and state to run that region.

Out of this group of Christians came the Anabaptist movement. While the other Reformers saw all of "Christendom" as Christian, they believed that just because people loosely identified themselves with the Church did not make them Christians. The Anabaptist movement wasn't organized but was a loose affiliation of people who held the same basic views that Christianity was based on a person's relationship with Jesus Christ.

Even to the other Reformers their views were held with contempt. The Catholics hated them as dangerous heretics. They found themselves persecuted in Protestant controlled areas because they thought their ideas threatened the religious stability of those regions. Many of the most pious followers of the Reformers followed the Anabaptists, going deeper into Christianity than most of the Reformers were willing to plunge. For twenty-five years thousands of these passive Christians were burned to death in Catholic-held territories and drowned to death in Protestant-held territories. What the Protestants did to the Anabaptists is an ugly reminder of what happens when Christianity is mixed with the power of government.

WEEK 8: OVERCOMING THE FLESH

Monday   THE SINFUL MIND

MEMORY VERSE: ROMANS 8:6

Look up the following verses about the human mind. For each one, tell what you learn about it.

1. Psalm 94:11

2. Proverbs 15:26

3. Jeremiah 4:14

4. Matthew 15:19

5. I Corinthians 2:12-14

6. Titus 1:15

1. Read Romans 1:24-32 and answer the following questions.

    a. According to verse 24, where did their lust originate?

    b. According to verse 24, what was the outcome to their own bodies through their behavior?

2. Look up the word "dishonor" in *Strong's* and *Vine's* and explain what you learn about it.

3. Now look up the other time this word is used in the New Testament (John 8:48-49). Consider the two uses of the word and describe in your own words what you think happens to a person who gives himself over to this kind of lifestyle.

4. Write out the three things listed in Romans 1:24-28 to which God gave them over.

    1.

    2.

    3.

5. According to Romans 1:29, these people were *filled* with these things. Look up the word "fill" in *Vine's* and give its definition.

6. Now read Matthew 5:6. Explain why these people were filled with righteousness.

7. In light of that verse, how would you describe the heartfelt desires of the people described in Romans 1?

8. List the nine things in verse 29 that these people's hearts are full of as they pursue a depraved lifestyle.

   1.   6.

   2.   7.

   3.   8.

   4.   9.

   5.

1. In Romans 7, we find the great chapter of Paul's personal struggle with his own sinful nature. The struggle comes into play because once we have come to know God, we begin striving to walk in obedience to His law. Unfortunately, however, our fleshly nature is still drawn to selfish and sinful desires. Read Romans 7:14-25 so that you can grasp the full weight of this struggle.

   Did you read it?

2. In chapter 7, Paul leaves us in what seems to be an impossible dilemma: God demanding perfection on the one hand but a sinful nature refusing to submit on the other. Read Romans 8:1-14 and answer the following questions.

   a. According to verses 1 and 2, why aren't we in condemnation?

   b. According to verse 3, how strong could the Law be in mortal man? Considering the dilemma we have been discussing, tell in your own words why your attempts to live in obedience to the law will always fall short?

   c. Read verse 3 & 4. God made provision for our sinfulness by sending His Son as an offering for our sins. According to verse 4, in whose life is the requirement of the Law fulfilled?

   d. Read verse 5-8. In each verse Paul says something about the person who lives his life in the flesh. Write them down.

      Verse 5:

      Verse 6:

      Verse 7:

      Verse 8:

In yesterday's study we saw that there is a battle between doing right and doing wrong in the mind of the Christian. We saw that we aren't strong enough in ourselves to live in obedience to God. And yet we also found that there are grave consequences if we don't.

1. Look at the illustration given below. Write out each of the verses listed in the spot given.

    The Law of God

    Romans 7:22

    The Law of Sin

    Romans 7:23

2. Too many people leave the quotient there. We often mistakenly think that this is the battle: the desire to do good (obey the Law of God) against the desire to do bad (obey the law of sin). But in Romans 8:1, Paul introduces the key to the whole problem. He says, "There is therefore now no condemnation for those who are *in* Christ Jesus." Read John 15:1-10 and answer the following questions.

    a. According to verses 2 & 6, what happens to those branches who don't bear fruit?

    b. According to verse 5, how much can a person do apart from Christ?

    c. According to verse 2, what does the Father do with the branch that does bear fruit?

    d. According to verses 5 & 7, what blessings are promised to those who abide in Christ?

    e. According to verse 8, what is the outcome of bearing fruit?

    f. According to verse 10, how will we abide in His love?

1. According to Romans 8, the key to overcoming sin is to have our minds set on the Spirit. You see, if we are not walking in the Spirit, we cannot please God, *even if we are trying to obey the Law of God!* We can only please God when our lives are hidden in Christ, in His Spirit. Write out Romans 8:8.

2. Read Galatians 5:16-26 and answer the following questions.

   a. According to verse 16, if you walk in the Spirit, what does Paul promise?

   b. In verse 17, we see an overview of the battle discussed in Romans 7. What does the flesh set against the Spirit?

   c. According to verse 18, what is the reward for being lead by the Spirit?

   d. Discuss this verse in light of John 15.

   In verses 19-21, we find the same type of lifestyle that was discussed in Romans 1. But in verses 22 & 23, we find a different lifestyle discussed. This is a lifestyle that is very pleasing to God but cannot be done in our own strength. As we learn to stay in constant communion with the Lord throughout the day and as we learn to crucify "the flesh with its passions and desires" (vs. 24), we begin to gradually walk more and more in the Spirit.

3. If we attempt to obey the Law outside of the Spirit, we will soon find ourselves becoming hard-hearted, self-righteous and contemptuous of others. Read Luke 18:9-14 again and tell in your own words how you think you can become an empty vessel who the Holy Spirit can fill, possess and bear fruit in.

Jeanne La Mothe lived in France during the prosperous reign of Louis XIV. Raised in a rich, affluent family, the beautiful young girl soon became a vain "butterfly," flitting around the Paris social scene of the seventeenth century. As a young teen she had had an experience with God but it soon fell by the way-side in her pursuit of the worldly lifestyle.

It all began to unravel for her when a wealthy man sought her hand in marriage. She reluctantly gave in to her father's wishes and agreed to marry him. Jacques Guyon was a good man, but allowed his mother to rule the house with a rod of iron. Young Jeanne's life soon became unbearable under the tyranny of her mother-in-law. She later could see God's merciful hand in the situation and said, "Such was the strength of my natural pride that nothing but some dispensation of sorrow would have broken down my spirit, and turned me to God."

But her plight at home was only the beginning of woes for her. About a year after her marriage a little boy was born to her but then one calamity after another befell her. First, her husband lost a great deal of his wealth; further agitating the temper of her mother-in-law. Then she became so sick that it looked as though she would die. No sooner had she gotten over the sickness than her beloved sister died; and then her mother. Now she turned to God to find solace in her miserable condition.

Later she would utter the following prayer to God about this time in her life. "Thou hast ordered these things, O my God, for my salvation! In goodness Thou hast afflicted me. Enlightened by the result, I have since clearly seen, that these dealings of Thy providence were necessary, in order to make me die to my vain and haughty nature." It was during this time that she came to know Christ in a definite way. After her born again experience she says: "Nothing was more easy to me now than to practice prayer. Hours passed away like moments, while I could hardly do anything else but pray. The fervency of my love allowed me no intermission. It was a prayer of rejoicing and of possession, wherein the taste of God was so great, so pure, so unblended and uninterrupted, that it drew and absorbed the powers of the soul into a profound recollection, a state of confiding and affectionate rest in God, existing without intellectual effort."

About a year after this experience, a second son was born to her, and then a daughter. While she grew deeper into the things of God, the pleasure-loving people she had been so a part of began to persecute and ridicule her for her faith in God. Her mother-in-law also became even more venomous in her attacks. Then at the age of twenty-two, in 1670, she was stricken with smallpox. The disease destroyed her beauty. Nevertheless, she said, "But the devastation without was counterbalanced by peace within. My soul was kept in a state of contentment, greater than can be expressed." While everyone around her thought that she would be inconsolable she said, "As I lay in my bed, suffering the total deprivation of that which had been a snare to my pride, I experienced a joy unspeakable. I praised God with profound silence."

As she got over this affliction, she was stricken with yet more. Within two years her youngest son, her daughter and her father all died. Then, not long after all of these, her best friend also died. And a couple of years after that, her husband died. Through all of this she had only praise for her God. "Oh, adorable conduct of my God! There must be no guide, no prop for the person whom Thou art leading into the regions of darkness and death."

During the next few years, Madam Guyon grew ever deeper into the riches of God's grace. As time went on, people started hearing about the woman in Paris who had lost so much, and yet who loved God all the more for it. One biographer wrote of her, "Madam Guyon's life was now characterized by great simplicity and power... And now, since she had received a deeper, richer, fuller experience herself, she began to lead many others into the experience of sanctification through faith, or into an experience of 'victory over the self life,' or 'death to the self life,' as she was fond of calling it. Her soul was all ablaze with the unction and power of the Holy Spirit, and everywhere she went she was besieged by multitudes of hungry, thirsty souls, who flocked to her for the spiritual meat that they failed to get from their regular pastors. Revivals in religion began in almost every place visited by her, and all over France earnest Christians began to seek the deeper experience taught by her."[4]

So many were led to renounce their worldliness and sinful behavior that worldly-minded priests began to vigorously persecute her. Soon the outcry against her became so intense that the king had her thrown into prison. Her first prison sentence lasted only eight months, but while there her enemies managed to poison her. She suffered for seven years from the effects of the poison. Lawson tells of this time: "Her writings were now sold and read all over France, and in many other parts of Europe, and in this way multitudes were brought to Christ and into a deeper spiritual experience through her teachings. In 1695 she was again imprisoned by order of the King, and this time was placed in the Castle of Vincennes. The following year she was transferred to a prison at Vaugiard. In 1698 she was placed in a dungeon in the Bastille, the historic and dreaded prison of Paris. For four years she was in this dungeon, but so great was her faith in God, her prison seemed like a palace to her. In 1702 she was banished to Blois, where she spent the remainder of her life in her Master's service. She died in perfect peace, and without a cloud on the fullness of her hopes and joy, in the year 1717, at 69 years of age."[5]

WEEK 9: OVERCOMING LIFE DOMINATING PROBLEMS

Monday   ANGER

MEMORY VERSE: GALATIANS 5:22-23

In last week's study we found that the answer to overcoming problems is to *walk in the Spirit*. People have often come to Pure Life wanting only to deal with their habits of sexual sin; not realizing that sexual sin isn't the underlying problem, but the whole selfish lifestyle outlined in Galatians 5:19-21. Keep this in mind as you do this week's studies about overcoming problems.

Look up the following verses and tell what you learn about anger.

1. Proverbs 25:28

2. Proverbs 29:22

3. Proverbs 30:33

4. Proverbs 12:16

5. Proverbs 14:29

6. Proverbs 19:11

Fear is an emotion given to us by God that operates in much the same manner as pain. Pain sends an alarm through the body that something is wrong and needs to be dealt with. Fear sends an alarm throughout the body that there is danger. But God has made provision for fear. The writer of Hebrews (quoting the Old Testament) said, "for He Himself has said, 'I will never desert you, nor will I ever forsake you,' so that we confidently say, 'The Lord is my helper, I will not be afraid. What shall man do to me?'"

With God on our side, who or what can be against us? We are in the hands of the Almighty. But you say, "Bad things happen to Christian too." That is very true. But when you truly learn to walk in the Spirit, you will not be dominated by fear.

1. Read the following verses and tell what you learn about fear.

   a. Romans 8:15

   b. Psalm 27:1

   c. Psalm 56:10-11

   d. Matthew 10:28-30

   e. II Timothy 1:7

2. Many who are dominated by fear see themselves as victims. As much as these people need compassion for their problem though, the fact is that fear has no hold on the person who isn't wrapped up in himself. A person who is truly putting God first in life and is more concerned with the welfare of others than he is about himself, is not going to be dominated by fear. Read I John 4:18 and explain in your own words what this means.

1. Anxiety is the stressful condition that comes about from a person who has not learned to put his trust in God. Read the following verses and tell what you have learned about worry and anxiety.

   a. Proverbs 12:25

   b. Proverbs 14:30

   c. Proverbs 17:22

   d. Matthew 6:25-34

2. Read Philippians 4:4-9 and answer the following questions.

   a. According to verses 4 & 6, what should you do instead of worrying?

   b. According to verse 8, what should you let your mind dwell on?

   c. According to verse 9, what should you do with the things you have learned here?

   d. According to verse 7, what will be the outcome of this kind of lifestyle?

1. There is a difference between discouragement and depression. Discouragement can happen to anybody, including the most Spirit-filled person. Depression, on the other hand, is the ongoing, self-centered gloom that a person allows himself to wallow in. It generally revolves around self-pity over one's circumstances. The same section of Scripture that we read yesterday applies here as well. As we learn to rejoice in all things, and focus our mind on godly things, we will not stay in a depressed state. Read II Corinthians 11:23-28.

Did you read it?

2. Now in light of all that Paul went through, read II Corinthians 4:8-9, and explain in your own words why we should never allow ourselves to fall into periods of depression.

3. Another thing that feeds depression is the guilt associated with unconfessed sin. Read Psalm 32:1-5. David was writing of what he went through after he had committed adultery with Bathsheba, but had not yet confessed. Explain what you think happened.

4. The last thing that encourages depression is having to deal with the consequences of sinful behavior and attitudes. In Genesis chapter four we find the story of Cain and Abel. Abel had brought an offering to the Lord that was pleasing in His sight. Cain, on the other hand, had brought an offering that he knew wouldn't be acceptable. Read verses 1-10 and answer the following questions.

   a. According to verse 5, what happened to Cain's countenance when he got angry with God?

   b. Explain God's answer to Cain's depression in verse 7?

   c. How did Cain end up handling the situation?

1. Laziness is the refusal to be diligent in life. Apathy is spiritual laziness. Read the following sections of Scripture and write what you have learned about laziness.

    a. Proverbs 20:4

    b. Proverbs 12:11

    c. Proverbs 6:6-11

    d. Proverbs 24:30-34

    e. Proverbs 26:13-16

    f. II Thessalonians 3:6-15

2. Now, having learned about laziness, draw correlations to your own spiritual life.

The pioneer of the modern-day missionary movement was born in England in 1761. William Carey became a shoemaker as a young man but upon receiving Christ, he soon became very serious about the things of God. As a young Christian, Carey came across the writings of the famous explorer, Captain Cook. Young William became fascinated with the idea of taking the Gospel to these faraway lands. He and a couple of friends formed a "mission society" to study the idea of taking the Gospel to India. When they tried to take this idea to the local minister's meeting, they were ridiculed to scorn. They remained undaunted.

Before long William met a Mr. John Thomas, a doctor who had traveled to India. He offered to take young Carey with him back there. Carey accepted without hesitation. Not long before this William had married a young English girl. She knew of his heart for missions but when he announced that he was going to India, she refused to go or let their children go. But this wasn't to be all of the opposition he would face. His father wrote him a scathing letter rebuking him for such a foolhardy idea. But he knew that God was calling him so he continued to go forward. He and Thomas traveled to London to try to book passage to India. While there, he wrote the following to his wife in a letter dated May 6, 1793:

> "If I had all the world, I would freely give it all to have you and my children with me, but the sense of duty is so strong as to overpower all other considerations. I cannot turn back without guilt on my soul."

As the two attempted to book passage, they ran into problem after problem. During the interim, his wife finally agreed to go with him. Once that happened, God miraculously provided and the small party was soon on their way. Six months later they arrived in Calcutta. Carey wrote in his journal, "I feel something of what Paul felt when he beheld Athens and 'his spirit was stirred within him.'"

But things did not go easy for them. The modern missionary movement was not going to be launched without many problems and demonic opposition. Within a few months, their money was gone. Mrs. Carey and their son both became seriously ill. One of his biographers tells of their plight: "They were in a strange country where they could scarcely speak the language. They were penniless, without food; Mrs. Carey was sick. There were the helpless children, and the little baby."[6] But God intervened and the small band of people finally established themselves.

The first few years in India took its toll on the family. From the beginning his wife was unable to handle the hardships they encountered. She gradually began losing touch with reality. Things became even worse when their young son died. As if all of this wasn't discouraging enough, it was over seven years—seven years of hard work—before Carey had his first convert.

Nevertheless, he continued to press forward. Eventually he was offered a position as the president of a college which afforded him more latitude and credibility than he had before. But even this was no guarantee that things would go smoothly. As other missionaries began arriving on the scene from England to help, they were denied entry by the government. After Carey put up a battle, the governor finally relented. But there was much pressure on the group not to try to win converts.

On December 7, 1807, Carey's wife died. "While this might have seemed like release from a burden, still it grieved him. He had loved Dorothy for many years. He had cared for and protected her as a father would a child, for her mind had been affected during most of the time they had been in India. Friends had wanted Carey to put her in an institution, but he could never bring himself to do this, for she was his wife, the mother of his children. To the end Carey treated her with the greatest love and respect."[7]

In 1809 William became deathly ill with a fever. He had worked tirelessly for years; teaching, preaching, running the mission, and his life's passion: translating the Bible into the many Indian languages and dialects. His body finally gave out.

But once again he overcame his obstacles and was soon back to work. He flung himself into his work with all the more passion. He translated all or parts of the Bible into the following languages and dialects: Bengali, Sanskrit, Orissa, Hindustani, Marathi, Sikh, Chinese, Pushtoo (Afghan), Kunkuna, Wuch, Assam, Bikaneer, Nepalese, Marwar, Kashmeer, Oojein, Jumboo, Kanoj, Khassee, Khosol, Bhutuneer, Dogura, Madjudha, Kumaoon and Judwal. It was an absolutely unbelievable feat for one man. True, he had helpers working on the various translations, but he still had to review and edit every single sentence to make sure that it was accurate. In 1825 Carey wrote, "The New Testament will soon be printed in thirty-four languages, and the Old Testament in eight, besides versions in three varieties of the Hindustani New Testament."

But his accomplishments did not come without severe setbacks. One of many happened in 1812 when a fire raced through their printing building. It was a devastation beyond description. Manuscripts and fonts that had taken years of hard work were lost. Although it was an unfathomable setback at the time, Carey wrote, "I wish to be still and know that the Lord He is God, and to bow to His will in everything. He will no doubt bring good out of this evil and make it promote His interests, but at present the providence is exceedingly dark."

Only in His providence can God know how these things will work out. None of them could have imagined what good could come out of such a calamity. But when news hit England of it, the Church leaped to their aid like never before. So much money started pouring in that in all good conscience they had to publish a statement saying that their needs had been met. But beyond this, it created a tremendous stir in England about his work.

Thus, with new help from home, he continued on his important work. It took several years to make up some of the lost work, but other projects were helped along the way. By his final days in life, William Carey had become full of the Personhood of Christ. George Gogerly, one of his contemporaries tells of visiting the old missionary days before his death.

"He was seated near his desk in the study, dressed in his usual neat attire. His eyes were closed and his hands clasped together... (His appearance) filled me with a kind of awe, for he seemed as one listening to his Master's summons, and ready to go. I sat there for about half an hour without a word, for I feared to break that silence, and to call back to earth the spirit that seemed almost in heaven. At last, however, I spoke, and well do I remember the very words that passed between us.

"'Dear friend,' said Gogerly, 'you seem to be standing on the very border of eternity. Do not think it wrong then that I ask your thoughts and feelings.'

"The question roused Dr. Carey. Slowly he opened his eyes, and then with a feeble though earnest voice he answered: *'I know in whom I have believed, and am persuaded that He is able to keep that which I have committed unto Him against that day. But when I think I am about to appear in God's holy presence, and I remember all my sins, I tremble.'*"[8]

Two days later William Carey did indeed go into his Savior's presence.

WEEK 10: CONTROLLING THE TONGUE

Monday   THE NEED FOR CONTROL

MEMORY VERSE: JAMES 1:26

1. Read the following verses and explain the importance of controlling our words.

   a. Psalm 19:14

   b. Proverbs 18:21

   c. I Peter 3:10

2. Read James 3:1-12 and answer the following questions.

   a. According to verse 1, how many should put themselves in the position of teaching others?

   b. According to verse 2, who is the perfect (mature) man?

   c. In verse 6 the tongue is called "a fire, the world of iniquity." Through our words, we can literally conjure up the vilest scenes. Explain why you think it is important that we don't talk of things we have done in the past, things of the world (movies, etc.), things that exalt carnality.

1. Many people talk without concerning themselves about what they are saying. Although they might not realize it, their idle chatter is just a self-centered means of bringing attention to themselves. Read the following verses and tell what you learn about idle words.

   a. I Peter 3:4

   b. Proverbs 18:2

   c. Proverbs 10:19

   d. Proverbs 17:27-28

   e. Matthew 12:36-37

2. Read Proverbs 12:23. Look up the word "folly" (foolishness KJV) in the *Strong's* and give the Hebrew word along with the definition. Then tell what you think this verse means.

3. Amy Carmichael once used the following criteria for speaking: "Is it true? Is it kind? Is it necessary?" We should be careful with what we say; not just in the sense that we shouldn't say unkind or deceitful things, but also that we shouldn't just talk to be talking. Explain in what ways you talk unnecessarily.

1. Read the following verses and tell what you learn about being argumentative.

   a. Proverbs 15:1

   b. Proverbs 12:18

   c. Proverbs 20:3

   d. Proverbs 17:14

   e. Ephesians 4:31-32

   f. I Peter 3:4

2. Read Colossians 4:5-6. There are many who are so bent on proving the truth of Christianity, or the wrongness of abortion, etc., that they argue with the unsaved to prove their point. In light of this verse, explain if you think this would be pleasing to God.

1. Look up the stories about the children of Israel whom Moses led out of Egypt and briefly describe what happened in each.

    a. Exodus 14:10-12

    b. Exodus 15:22-24

    c. Exodus 16:1-3

    d. Exodus 17:1-3

2. Look up the following verses about grumbling and tell what you learn.

    a. Proverbs 19:3

    b. Lamentations 3:39

    c. Philippians 2:14

1. Read I Timothy 1:5-7. According to verse 5, what one word describes the goal of Paul's instruction?

2. Read I Corinthians 8:1 and explain how these two verses might go together.

3. In I Corinthians 13, Paul says that love "does not seek its own." Can you see how many people use teaching as a self-centered way to bring attention to themselves, rather than really being concerned with the good of others? Have you ever been guilty of this? Explain.

4. Read verse 7 (I Timothy 1) and explain in your own words what it means.

5. Have you ever come across with great confidence about a subject, only to find out later that you were wrong? Tell about it.

6. Watchman Nee said, "Probably you yourself are the only one in the whole world who considers your opinion as the best. Persons with many opinions, ideas, and subjective thoughts are to be feared. They like to be counselors to all. They seize upon every opportunity to press their ideas on others. God can never use a person so full of opinions..."[9]

   Can you see the need to be careful about espousing your views?

7. Read I Timothy 3:6 (where Paul is laying out the qualifications for a leader) and tell how this verse could apply to you.

There has probably never been a missionary who has suffered more than Adoniram Judson, America's first foreign missionary. Born in 1788, he married Ann Hasseltine in 1812 and the two of them soon set sail for India. When they arrived, they found out that the government would not allow them to stay. It was the venerable old missionary William Carey who told them of the great need in Burma for the Gospel. But he warned them of the hardships they could expect, telling them of a priest who was beaten with an iron maul until he went insane. Nevertheless, the young couple was intent on going.

The first order of business was to master the Burmese language. But this proved to be a nightmare. He found that words stretched on endlessly, into sentences and even paragraphs. Adoniram ended up learning the Burmese language by the hardest way possible—pointing at objects and learning the sound of the accompanying word.

But, just as it had been for Carey in India, so the going was perhaps even harder for Adoniram and Ann. Not long after arriving, Ann got very sick. And then their baby boy died. At the same time, as Judson travailed over the Burmese language, his eyes began giving him excruciating headaches. He relentlessly continued his language study in spite of the pain. Then, three years after arriving in Rangoon, he finished his Burmese-English grammar.

As Judson learned the language he began preaching salvation. But to his discouragement, the people were too afraid of the authorities to listen to him. Ann's health problems also continued. She would get better for awhile, but soon the tropical climate would bring her down again. She was finally told that her only chance to survive was to take an extended trip back to America. Still, Judson continued his work.

It was two and a half years later before he would see his beloved wife. Not long after arriving back, Adoniram was arrested for spying. The British had just invaded Burma and anybody with white skin was suspect. He was tossed into prison, but even though he had been in Burma for several years, nothing could have prepared him for what he would experience there. "Every nerve shrank from the frightful smell of the squalid place...The floor was mat-ted with rotting animals, human filth, the infernal betel juice spit from the drooling mouths of a thousand or more prisoners."[10] For over two years Adoniram stayed in this prison, kept alive by eating vermin. During this whole time his beloved Ann persistently pestered every government official who would listen to release her husband. When he finally did get out, he came home to find her nothing more than a rack of bones, near death from sickness and exhaustion. He nursed her back to health but she soon had a relapse. At the age of thirty-seven, Ann Judson died.

Adoniram was heartbroken beyond words. He fanatically threw himself into his work, to the edge of insanity. And then, six months later, his third child died. Still he continued relentlessly on. He worked on his Burmese translation of the Bible, preached at every opportunity, wrote tracts in Burmese and continued to work with his small handful of converts. Then, after sixteen years in Burma, suddenly people began to get saved! For some time it was as if he could do nothing wrong. People began seeking him out to hear about salvation. His tracts were being distributed all over Burma. During this time another missionary couple had arrived, but soon the husband died. Three years later Adoniram married Sarah Boardman, the widow.

After twenty-two years of work in Burma, Judson developed a sharp pain in his throat that would stay with him the rest of his life. The tropical climate had destroyed his lungs and throat. Since he had to reluctantly agree to quit preaching, he took up the monumental task of developing a Burmese dictionary. This would prove to be invaluable to those missionaries who would follow him to this harsh, forgotten land.

After ten years of marriage and several children, his second beloved wife succumbed to sickness. Once again Adoniram buried his heartache in his work. He worked on tirelessly for another five years, when at the age of sixty-two, the battered old veteran missionary finally went home to his many rewards. Adoniram Judson suffered much for the sake of Christ. The loss of loved ones, constant bouts of sickness, deprivation and persecution had been his lifelong companions. But from the life he poured out, thousands were able to eventually come to Christ.

WEEK 11: SPEAKING TRUTH

Monday   DELUSION

MEMORY VERSE: JOHN 14:6

Vine's Expository Dictionary defines *delusion* (Greek *planē*) as, "literally, a wandering, whereby those who are led astray roam hither and thither, is always used in the New Testament of mental straying, wrong opinion, error in morals or religion."[11]

Being a deceitful person always begins with self-deception. About the deluded person David said, "...There is no fear of God before his eyes. For in his own eyes he flattereth himself too much to detect and hate his own sin" (Psalm 36:1-2 NIV). When we "pump ourselves up," all we do is overlook our own sin. The outcome of this arrogant thinking is a lack of fear of God. When we really walk in truth, we see our sin, mourn over it, and fear God because it is displeasing to Him. When we are deluded, we discount or minimize our sin and therefore have little fear of God.

Look up the following verses and tell what you learn about what brings delusion into a person's life. Also, tell how each of these things has affected you or brought delusion about in your life.

1. Matthew 13:22

2. James 1:22

3. Hebrews 3:13

4. Galatians 6:3

Read the following verses and tell what you learn about being truthful.

1. Joshua 24:14

2. Psalm 51:6

3. Jeremiah 5:3

4. John 3:21

5. John 8:32

6. I Corinthians 13:6

7. Ephesians 4:25

8. I John 1:8

1. Read John 8:44 and list the five characteristics of deception given about Satan.

    1.

    2.

    3.

    4.

    5.

There have been those who have wondered about some of Satan's actions, considering that he knows what the final outcome will be: that he will be cast into the lake of fire! But what most people don't know is how eaten up with delusion Satan and his demons are. You can't practice deceit without being deceived yourself. Satan and his fallen angels are in deep delusion about reality. They actually believe they can win this war! That's why he and his followers will attack the Lord in the Battle of Armageddon.

Deception begets more deception. We all must be extremely careful to be honest with ourselves in every area of life.

2. Read the following verses and tell what you learn about deception.

    a. Psalm 101:7

    b. Proverbs 12:22

    c. Proverbs 19:9

    d. Jeremiah 17:9

3. How often do you deceive yourself or others? Prayerfully answer this question.

Flattery is the use of excessive and ingratiating praise toward another for the purpose of manipulation. People love to be encouraged. What many do, though, is attempt to "pump others up," not for the sake of encouragement, but either to appease or to promote their own self-interests. Exhortation is the gift of encouraging someone to do the right thing. Mercy is the gift of coming alongside someone who is hurting. Both of these gifts are born out of a heart of love and have the *other* person's good at stake. Flattery, on the contrary, is self-centered and has the person's *own* good at stake.

1. Look up the following verses and tell what you learn about flattery.

   a. Psalm 12:3

   b. Proverbs 24:24

   c. Proverbs 28:23

   d. Proverbs 29:5

   e. I Thessalonians 2:5

2. How have you, or do you, use flattery in your own life? Give illustrations.

1. Read the following verses and tell what you learn about gossip.

   a. Proverbs 11:9

   b. Proverbs 16:28

   c. Proverbs 18:8

   d. James 4:11-12

2. God's people are called the "apple" of His eye. The Bible says He loves us so much He sent His own Son to die on our behalf. Even if we have deluded ourselves into thinking otherwise, He does not think highly of those who talk against His people—especially His servants. Read the story in Numbers 12 and tell what you learn from it.

3. How often do you talk about others? Can you see that gossip is for the purpose of trying to make ourselves look better at someone else's expense? Explain what kind of a problem this is in your life. Give illustrations.

David Livingstone, the great missionary/explorer who opened up the dark continent of Africa, was born in Scotland in 1813. By this time Carey had already been in India a number of years and Judson was just beginning his work in Burma. But Livingstone wasn't to arrive at his mission field until the year 1841.

Livingstone hadn't been in Africa but a couple of years before his first of many brushes with death occurred. He was ministering in an area that was being plagued with lions. As he was hunting one day he ran across one and shot it. But before he could reload again it attacked him. "The lion caught me by the shoulder and we both came to the ground together. Growling horribly, he shook me as a terrier does a rat. The shock produced a stupor similar to that which seems to be felt by a mouse after the first grip of the cat."[12] The lion then turned on two others traveling with Livingstone before it finally succumbed to the bullets. The bone in Livingstone's left arm was shattered and was maimed for the rest of his life.

David Livingstone's great calling was to open up Africa for others to follow him. While he stayed with tribes and preached Christ continually, he had very little in the way of immediate results. His was a pioneering mission. And, while Christian missionaries did follow him later, his efforts were used at the time by Satan in a terrible way. Slave traders were at this time scouring Africa looking for victims to haul off to America and Europe. Livingstone had tremendous success with the tribes because they could see that he was indeed a sincere and loving man. But no sooner did Livingstone open up a trail into a new region than the murderous slave traders would follow in his footsteps; often claiming to be his children! This made many Africans distrust even Livingstone's motives. "It is hard" says he, "to work for years with pure motives, and all the time be looked on by most of those to whom our lives are devoted, as having some sinister object in view."[13]

But regardless of the enemy's efforts to discourage him, Livingstone's great call was exploration. In his thirty-three years of service in Africa, he is said to have traveled some 29,000 miles—mostly on foot through thick jungle! His efforts made known some million square miles of previously uncharted land. He discovered lakes N'gami, Shirwa, Nyassa, Moero and Bangweolo. He also discovered the upper Zambesi River and the marvelous Victoria Falls.

In the year 1862 Livingstone's wife died of the dreaded African fever. Of this he wrote in his journal: "It is the first heavy stroke I have suffered, and quite takes away my strength. I wept over her who well deserved many tears. I loved her when I married her, and the longer I lived with her I loved her the more. God pity the poor children, who were all tenderly attached to her; and I am left alone in the world by one whom I felt to be a part of myself. I hope it may, by divine grace, lead me to realize heaven as my home, and that she has but preceded me in the journey. Oh, my Mary, my Mary; how often we have longed for a quiet home... For the first time in my life I feel willing to die."[14]

Still, he pressed on. Taking journeys into the interior time after time; looking for new tribes of peoples to share Christ with. But these important trips didn't come without great sacrifice and suffering. Livingstone would travel for months, literally too sick to walk. His men would carry him through the jungle. The following journal entry is but one of many that showed the typical price he paid to take the precious Gospel to the unsaved:

"January 27th. In changing my dress this A.M. I was frightened at my own emaciation.

"April 1st, '67. I am excessively weak; can not walk without tottering, and have constant singing in the head, but the Highest will lead me further... After I had been a few days here I had a fit of insensibility, which shows the power of fever without medicine. I found myself floundering outside my hut, and, unable to get in, I tried to lift myself from my back by laying hold of two posts at the entrance, but when I got nearly upright I let them go, and fell back heavily on my head on a box."[15]

Livingstone continued on for several more years; some years spent more months sick with the fever than well. After many years of selfless service for his Master, David Livingstone died of the fever in the jungle at the age of sixty-two.

WEEK 12: FINDING SELF FULFILLMENT

Monday   THE REIGN OF SOLOMON

MEMORY VERSE: MATTHEW 6:33

1. Read I Kings 3:1-15 and describe what happened. What weak spot do you see in Solomon's life that eventually helped lead to his downfall?

2. Read I Kings 11:1-14 and describe what happened in your own words.

1. King Solomon was richer than any other Jewish king. In each of the following verses in the book of Ecclesiastes, write down the thing that Solomon used to try to find fulfillment.

    a. 1:16-18

    b. 2:1

    c. 2:2

    d. 2:3

    e. 2:4-6

    f. 2:7

    g. 2:8

    h. 2:9

2. Write out 2:10-11.

3. According to verses 17 and 18 in chapter two, what was Solomon's final feeling about life after having all of the things listed above?

4. After having reviewed Solomon's life, why do you think he ended up dying a miserable old man?

In Exodus chapter three, we find the story of God revealing Himself to Moses through a burning bush. When Moses asked the Lord who he should say sent him, the Lord told him to tell them that "I AM WHO I AM" sent you. God revealed Himself as "I AM"

I believe that God is saying, "I am the God who will supply every need and give you true and lasting fulfillment in life. But you will not find that if you search for fulfillment outside of Me; you will find only emptiness and futility."

You see, we all seem to be born with a vacuum of sorts in our souls. This is an empty spot in the heart that I believe God created us with. Unfortunately, people try to fill this empty spot with all kinds of things: drugs, alcohol, gambling, hobbies, relationships, illicit sex, etc. But to put anything before God's rightful place in our lives is nothing short of idolatry, whether it be an addiction or something as innocuous as a nice home for your family. *God must be first in our lives and will never accept second place!*

1. Write out Philippians 4:19

2. Read Exodus 20:1-6 and answer the following questions about the Ten Commandments.

    a. As the Lord identifies Himself in verse 2, what are the first two words He speaks?

    b. Write out verse 3.

    c. According to verse 5, what does God say about Himself?

    d. According to verse 5, what does God say an idolatrous person feels about Him?

    e. According to verse 5, what happens to these people?

    f. According to verse 6, what does He do to those who love Him and keep His commandments?

Read the following verses and tell what you learn about finding your fulfillment in God.

1. Psalm 37:4

2. Psalm 63:1-5

3. Psalm 107:9

4. Matthew 11:28-30

5. John 4:14

6. John 15:11

7. Ephesians 3:19

8. Ephesians 5:18

Write out the nine fruits of the Spirit found in Galatians 5:22-23. For each one, describe what it would mean to you to demonstrate it on an ongoing basis in your life.

1.

2.

3.

4.

5.

6.

7.

8.

9.

Hudson Taylor, the man with the heart for China, was born in England in 1832. As a young man, Taylor sensed the call of God on his life to the mission field. He entered medical school and spent the next several years being prepared for the Master's service. But, unlike so many others who answer that call with a partial response, young Hudson took this matter very seriously. He says of this time:

"Having now the twofold object in view of accustoming myself to endure hardness, and of economizing in order to be able more largely to assist those among whom I spent a good deal of time laboring in the Gospel, I soon found that I could live upon very much less than I had previously thought possible. Butter, milk, and other such luxuries I soon ceased to use; and I found that by living mainly on oatmeal and rice, with occasional variations, a very small sum was sufficient for my needs. In this way I had more than two-thirds of my income available for other purposes; and my experience was that the less I spent on myself and the more I gave away, the fuller the happiness and blessing did my soul become. Unspeakable joy all the day long, and every day, was my happy experience. God, even my God, was a living, bright reality; and all I had to do was joyful service.

"It was to me a very grave matter, however to contemplate going out to China, far away from all human aid, there to depend upon the living God alone for protection, supplies, and help of every kind. I felt that one's spiritual muscles required strengthening for such an undertaking."[16]

Hudson continued on with his studies, working tirelessly both at a job and in service for the Lord. But the call on his life would be severely tested. While still in London he came down with a dreaded disease and spent months so sick that he could barely manage to get out of bed. He finally got better and the time was at hand to sail for China. But no sooner had the schooner set out to sea than she was buffeted by a savage storm. The ship was tossed to and fro until it was a stone's throw from a rocky shore line. But even through this Taylor had a peace that God's hand was in control and that everything would be alright. At the last possible moment the

winds relented and the ship made it out to sea. Several months later, in 1854, young Hudson Taylor stepped off the ship into the city of Shanghai.

Hudson was able to stay with another missionary for several months while learning the difficult Chinese language. During this time, he quickly found out how unstable China was. As he showed up in Shanghai, the city was being sieged and fought over by rival bands of rebels. During one battle, two coolies who were traveling with him were killed by a cannon ball. Another time a cannon ball missed him by inches. But Hudson Taylor was on a mission for God and was being protected by His mighty hand.

But God doesn't always protect His precious servants from adversity. On one evangelistic trip to another city, Taylor and his traveling companion were warned not to enter the city as they would most surely be killed by the soldiers there. They felt that God sent them there so they went anyway. As they walked into the city, people began calling them names, but otherwise didn't bother them. Taylor tells what happened next:

"Long before we reached the gate, however, a tall powerful man, made ten-fold fiercer by partial intoxication, let us know that all the militia were not so peaceably inclined, by seizing Mr. Burdon by the shoulders. My companion endeavored to shake him off. I turned to see what was the matter, and at once we were surrounded by a dozen or more brutal men, who hurried us on to the city at a fearful pace.

"My bag began to feel very heavy, and I could not change hands to relieve myself. I was soon in a profuse perspiration, and was scarcely able to keep pace with them. We demanded to be taken before the chief magistrate, but were told that they knew where to take us, and what to do with such persons as we were, with the most insulting epithets. The man who first seized Mr. Burdon soon afterward left him for me, and became my principal tormentor; for I was neither so tall nor so strong as my friend, and was therefore less able to resist him. He all but knocked me down again and again, seized me by the hair, took hold of my collar so as to almost choke me, and grasped my arms and shoulders, making them black and blue.

Had this treatment continued much longer, I must have fainted. [17]

At last they were taken to a magistrate's office and were then treated with more respect. The magistrate felt so badly about the abuse they had endured that he sent men with them to protect them as they preached and passed out literature! Thus, God was able to use Satan's attack to spread the Gospel.

Taylor spent the next several years preaching at every opportunity, passing out literature and showing his willingness to suffer for the cause of Christ. But just as he felt his work was being blessed by the Lord, he became deathly sick and eventually was forced to return to England. It was a heartbreaking setback for one with a passion for souls. In his time there, he had developed a real passion to reach the interior of China where no other missionaries had gone. Now it seemed that all his plans and hopes were aborted. In great discouragement he made the long journey back to England.

His heart was still in China, however. As he slowly began to recuperate in England, he found himself having opportunities to share his vision for taking the Gospel into the inner parts of China. But he was afraid to share his vision out of fear that those who would respond might be killed over there.

"Yet, what was I to do? The feeling of blood-guiltiness became more and more intense. Simply because I refused to ask for them, the laborers did not come forward—did not go out to China—and every day tens of thousands were passing away to Christless graves. Perishing China so filled my heart and mind that there was no rest by day, and little sleep by night, till health broke down...

"On Sunday, June 25, 1865, unable to bear the sight of a congregation of a thousand or more Christian people rejoicing in their own security, while millions were perishing for lack of knowledge, I wandered out on the sands alone, in great spiritual agony; and there the Lord conquered my unbelief, and I surrendered myself to God for this service.[18]

Satan had meant his sickness for evil but God had used it for His own purposes. Out of his trip back to England came the formation of the China Inland Mission. For the next forty years God used Hudson Taylor and his followers to take the precious Gospel into the interior of China. Thousands would come to know Christ by their efforts, and maybe even more importantly, the interior of China was opened up for hundreds of other missionaries as well.

WEEK 13: REPENTING OF DOUBLE-MINDEDNESS

Monday   DOUBLE-MINDEDNESS

MEMORY VERSE: I JOHN 1:6-7

Look up the following verses and tell what you learn about being double-minded.

1. Joshua 24:14-15

2. I Kings 18:21

3. II Kings 17:33

4. Luke 16:13

5. I Corinthians 10:21

6. James 1:6-8

7. James 4:8

1. It is unfortunate but true that most American Christians really don't have a true appreciation for the price that was paid for their salvation. In our selfishness, we often delude ourselves into thinking that we can have Christianity and the old, carnal lifestyle at the same time. Write out I Corinthians 6:20 and describe what that price was.

2. Read I Corinthians 6:9-19 and answer the following questions.

   a. According to the first part of verse 9, who shall not inherit the kingdom of God?

   b. List the types of behavior listed of those who shall not inherit the kingdom of God.

      1.   6.

      2.   7.

      3.   8.

      4.   9.

      5.   10.

   c. In verse 11, list the three things that happen to the person who has truly been saved.

      1.

      2.

      3.

   d. According to verses 15 & 16, we should not join ourselves together with a harlot. In each of the following verses, Paul gives us a reason why we shouldn't. List them.

      1. Verse 17:

      2. Verse 18:

      3. Verse 19a:

      4. Verse 19b-20:

Many people continue to live in sin after making a profession of faith to follow Christ. Look up the following verses and tell what you learn about those who continue in sin.

1. Matthew 7:21

2. Romans 8:13

3. Galatians 5:19-21

4. Ephesians 5:5-6

5. Hebrews 10:26

6. I John 1:6

7. I John 2:4

Look up the following verses about staying "in the faith" and about what happens to those who commit apostasy. Tell what you learn about it. (Notice how many times the word "if" is used.)

1. Jeremiah 2:13-19

2. Romans 11:22

3. Colossians 1:21-23

4. Hebrews 3:6, 12-14

5. Hebrews 10:35-39

6. II Peter 1:10-11

7. II Peter 2:20-22

8. Revelation 3:5

1. Jesus and Paul both warned that in the last days there would be many who "fall away" from the faith. Look up the following verses and tell what you learn about those days.

    a. Matthew 24:10-13

    b. Matthew 24:24

    c. II Thessalonians 2:3

2. Read the two sections of Scripture listed below and tell how you think the spirit of the anti-christ might be able to deceive "even the elect."

    a. II Thessalonians 2:8-12

    b. Revelation 13:13-14

3. I recently heard a message from Romans 12:2 by a minister for whom I have tremendous respect. He said that God is trying to transform our "fallen" minds into the mind of Christ. Although the anti-christ wasn't the topic of his message, he made a very poignant statement that bears repeating. He said that those who continually watch television are keeping their minds within the mentality of this world. He said that one day a man would appear on that television claiming to have all of the answers for the problems of mankind. He went on to say that Christians often naively think that they will be able to withstand the deception of the anti-christ when he comes, but those who watch television are at present aligning their minds with him already. He said it would be *impossible* for them to withstand the heavy delusion that will come upon the world that day. He said this: "If they can't say 'no' to that television now, what makes them think they will be able to say 'no' to it when that day comes?"

Look up the word "transform" in a dictionary, and write out its definition. Then describe it in context of our minds being transformed from the thinking of this world into the thinking of real Christianity.

Although not a house-hold name, Jonothan Goforth's life in China is a prime example of a life given over to the Savior's will. Born in Canada in 1859, Jonothan and his wife, Rosalind, didn't arrive in Shanghai, China until the year 1888. The young couple hadn't been there but a few days when a fire broke out in the house they were staying in and burned up almost all of their belongings. While it was a mere temporary setback for Jonothan, to be endured with his customary cheerfulness, it meant the burning of the bridges for Rosalind in regard to material possessions.

After several months of language study, the Goforths were allowed to set out for their assignment: North Honan. The venerable old missionary (by now) Hudson Taylor wrote the Goforths a letter in which he said, "Brother, if you would enter that Province, you must go forward on your knees."[19]

Several months after arriving there, dysentery broke out among some of the workmen and then the Goforths' little daughter became ill. She died within a week. "None but those who have lost a precious treasure can understand our feelings, but the loss seems to be greater because we are far away in a strange land... We pray that this loss will fit us more fully to tell these dying millions of Him who has gained the victory over death."[20]

It wasn't but six months later that their little son faced tragedy. While racing around a second story porch, the little boy fell off onto the ground below, striking his head on a flower pot. Though at first there was no apparent injury, gradually he began losing the use of his limbs and a few months later died also. But the Goforths weren't living for themselves, but for the unsaved multitudes they had been called to reach.

Ministering was made difficult in China at this time by the great mistrust the people had for Caucasians. Wild stories were circulated about the missionaries that the "miracles" they worked with medicines must be made of something precious. These troublemakers said that the "foreign devils" scooped out the eyes and cut out the hearts of children to manufacture their medicine. Placards were posted up all over the country calling for the death of all of the missionaries.

Preaching was very difficult as well. The missionaries would go into a city or village and draw a crowd by their presence and begin sharing Jesus with the people. Inevitably, someone behind them would kick them in the backside. The crowd would laughingly roar their approval. If the missionary made the mistake of turning around to see who did it, they would then be attacked by the others. Goforth learned that the key was to preach with his back to a wall, thus averting much of the problem.

After several years, the Goforths were allowed to go deeper into China; into Changte. White people were new to the people of this region and so the missionary family would have hundreds of visitors a day. Jonothan felt it to be of great importance to take advantage of this opportunity while they had it. So day after day, stretching into weeks, the Goforths would literally preach all day, everyday to the throngs who came. When exhaustion really began taking its toll, they started praying that God would send them help. And soon thereafter they were joined in the work by an old opium addict who had become radically saved.

In 1898 the Goforths' little girl Gracie came down with malaria and succumbed to it not long after. Then their little boy became ill with dysentery and measles. As he began recovering, his worn out father came down with a bad attack of jaundice. For weeks Jonothan lay seriously ill in bed. While this was going on, Mrs. Goforth, who was pregnant and also very worn out, went into childbirth. She almost died giving birth but eventually managed to recover.

It was two years later before calamity struck again. This time it was their eldest daughter, Florence, who was now seven years of age. She developed meningitis and died shortly thereafter. It wasn't but a few days later that an urgent message came from the American Consul in Chefoo to flee to the south. A nationalistic movement that had been building up for years finally erupted into what is now known as the "Boxer Rebellion." Foreigners across the country were being massacred.

The party of thirteen adults and five children (four of which were the Goforth's) set out in carts for the south immediately. Almost everywhere they went, they heard the shouts, "Kill! Kill!" Sometimes they were pelted with rocks, but for a time they managed to escape real harm. Then they came to a town where a crowd of several hundred men awaited them with arms full of stones and daggers in their belts. First a fusillade of stones came at them. Then some gunshots and a rush forward. The men attacked with a fury. Jonothan was struck several times with a sword, leaving gashes in his arm to the bone and one terrible one in the back of his head. As he lay on the ground, a man on a horse came at full gallop to trod him under foot but as Goforth looked up, suddenly the horse fell next to him and lay kicking furiously—creating a barrier between Goforth and his attackers.

As the small band of people tried to escape the mob, they were beaten and pelted with more rocks. The whole group managed to make it into one cart and got away from that mob only to run into another one. Word was sent to a local official that they desperately needed help. Soldiers were sent to protect them but it wasn't until later that they discovered the soldiers intended to massacre the small band of people themselves when they got to a certain place. As the band of Christians were riding in one cart and the soldiers in another, the soldiers fell asleep on the carts and, coming to a fork in the road, went the wrong way! Thus their lives were again spared.

Time and time again the little group was surrounded by wild mobs but strangely they were never again attacked. They finally made it to safety. Before long things calmed down in China and once again the missionaries were back to work. In 1902 the Goforths were given a region to evangelize that greatly excited Jonothan. He felt that the Lord gave him a plan that he would go to a city, open a center for the Gospel, start a church and establish leaders there, and then move on to another city. Mrs. Goforth, in her concern for her children, didn't share his enthusiasm, though. Jonothan pleaded with her to change her mind. He assured her that the safest place for the children was in the Lord's work. He even said that he was so sure this plan was of God

that he feared for the children if *she didn't obey.*

Then their little boy came down with a terrible case of Asiatic dysentery. Mrs. Goforth could only think of the four little graves they had already dug. She tells the story:

"For two weeks we fought for the child's life. During that time, my husband whispered to me gently, 'O Rose, give in before it is too late!' But I only thought him hard and cruel. Then, when Wallace began to recover, my husband packed up and left on a tour *alone.*

"The day after he left, my precious baby Constance was taken ill suddenly, as Wallace had been, only much worse. Constance was dying when Mr. Goforth arrived. My husband knelt next to Constance and I beside him. The little one was quietly passing when suddenly I saw in a strange and utterly new way the *love* of God—as a *Father.* All at once, as in a flash, I *knew* that my Heavenly Father could be trusted to keep my children! This all came so overwhelmingly upon me, I could only bow my head and say, 'O God, it is too late for Constance, but I will trust.'"[21] The Goforths continued ministering in China for over thirty more years, literally being used by God to bring a multitude of unsaved souls into the kingdom. Although it came at great sacrifice, in the eternal realm it was all worth it.

WEEK 14: THE WAY OF WISDOM

Monday   CARNAL KNOWLEDGE

MEMORY VERSE: COLOSSIANS 1:9-10

1. Last week, we studied the concept of having a double *mind*. This week, we will carry the study a bit further as we look at the human mind. In Friday's study, we talked about the day the anti-christ will come will bring with him a tremendous power of delusion, whereby he will be able to deceive even the elect. How will he accomplish this? By appealing to our fallen, carnal minds! Write out Proverbs 14:12.

2. Knowledge is a tricky and often elusive thing. Since our minds are part of our fallen nature, we can never be totally sure that we are right about anything—unless it is written in Scripture. Anything else is subject to the insanity of our fallen minds.

    How many times have you arrived at a conclusion—to the point of being willing to argue to prove it was true—only to find out later you were wrong? The fallen mind is a strange thing. At the time we arrive at a conclusion about something, it is what we believe. Because of our pride we refuse to accept the fact that we might not be right, so we stubbornly hold onto our beliefs.

    As we begin to grow and mature in Christ, some things we once *knew* to be true are proven to be false. The closer we come to Jesus, the more our minds become like His, and the more clearly we see reality for what it really is. Read the following verses and tell what you learn about knowledge, the heart, and the mind of sinful man.

    a. Matthew 15:19

    b. Romans 3:3-4

    c. Ephesians 4:17

3. Considering the Scriptures listed above, how trustworthy is your own thinking?

It's funny how our minds think. Have you ever noticed how your mind always tends toward thinking the best of yourself? Just to show you the truth of this, think back to the last time you had a disagreement with someone. Do you remember walking away from it rehearsing over and over in your mind *your points, your thoughts* and how *you were right?* Be honest: how much "air time" did you give the other person's points and ideas? Very little, right?

The truth is, we think more highly of our own opinions than anyone else. In fact, we *always* think we're right! If we didn't think we were right, we would think something else and we would think *that* was right!

A favorite saying of men who come into our live-in program is, "My best thinking got me here!" In other words, the best decisions and thinking he could do in life were so bad that he had to go to a live-in program to get his thinking squared away!

The fact is, we *want* to think we are always right and we always know the right thing to do. The beginning of humility is conceding the *fact* that we do not.

1. Write out Proverbs 12:15.

2. Another thing about knowledge is that the more we have of it, the more arrogant we become. Write out I Corinthians 8:1.

3. Now explain why you think knowledge would make a person "puffed up," but love would serve to edify others.

4. In our deluded thinking, we tend to build ourselves up *at the expense of God*. You see, the more you build yourself up, the more your pride causes you to stand in defiance of God. Read Proverbs 1:7 and explain how having a holy fear and reverence for God would tend to decrease your arrogant thinking.

5. David said, "There is no fear of God before his eyes. For in his own eyes he flatters himself too much to detect or hate his own sin." (Psa. 36:1-2 NIV). Explain this in the context of your own thinking.

1. As the Apostle Paul attempted to bring the Gospel to the Gentiles, he found that one of his biggest stumbling blocks was the philosophies that were so prevalent in his day. The word "philosophy" means nothing more than the ideas and concepts people hold about life. People who are "in the dark" cannot have true knowledge about life, however. In the Church in America today, we have allowed the philosophies of ungodly men to come into the Church under the guise of "science."

   Read I Corinthians 1:17 through 3:23 and explain any correlation you see between what Paul dealt with and what we deal with today.

2. Write out Colossians 2:8

3. In James 3:13-18 we find an examination of the difference between the world's wisdom in the Church and the wisdom of God in the Church. Read this passage and answer the following questions.

   a. According to verse 13, how does a person show godly wisdom?

   b. List the eight characteristics of godly wisdom given in verse 17.

   1.   5.

   2.   6.

   3.   7.

   4.   8.

   c. List the four characteristics of worldly wisdom given in verse 16.

   1.   3.

   2.   4.

4. Can you see how some teachers in the Church today appeal to the logic of the carnal mind in their own ambitious drive to fame and self-glory?

1. The last two hundred years have produced an absolute explosion of knowledge and information. Inventions have numbered in the millions. New ideas and concepts abound everywhere. In less than a hundred years we have gone from traveling in simple carts to sending a man to the moon!

    But this was all predicted by the prophet Daniel, who said that in the last days knowledge would greatly increase. This increase in knowledge has had a profound effect on Christians. We have sought it with reckless abandon. Our problem is that we haven't exercised wisdom in *what* we have acquired as knowledge. Write out Proverbs 14:15.

2. With biblical knowledge comes responsibility. We are responsible to *respond* to what we have been taught. In an earlier study we saw that it is dangerous to hear the Word of God if we don't live out what we have heard. The reason for that is that the more knowledge about Christ we have, the more like Christ we should become. If we refuse to *live* what we *learn*, we quickly go into deluded thinking about our own spirituality. In this age of knowledge, we tend to gauge our Christianity not on *what we live* – but on *what we know!*

    What makes this frightening is that our lives and behavior will be judged *against* how much *knowledge of the truth* we have received! When we stand before God, our knowledge will be what God uses to gauge our lives! Read the following verses and tell what you learn about this truth.

    a. Matthew 11:21-24

    b. Luke 12:42-48

    c. James 3:1

3. Explain why you think it is important to be careful about what you "learn."

1. Read Proverbs 1:1-4 and tell what the eight reasons are for the *Book of Proverbs*.

   1.   5.

   2.   6.

   3.   7.

   4.   8.

2. Write out James 1:5.

3. Read Proverbs 2:2-4. Tell what the six actions are of one who wants God's wisdom.

   1.   4.

   2.   5.

   3.   6.

4. Read Proverbs 2:5-12. Explain in your own words what God's wisdom will do for you.

5. Go through the book of Proverbs and pick out ten instructions that you would consider words of wisdom for your own life.

   1.   6.

   2.   7.

   3.   8.

   4.   9.

   5.   10.

Taiyuan, the capital of Shansi Province in China, became the scene of one of the bloodiest massacres of modern-day Christianity. This happened because Yu-hsien, one of the chief conspirators of the Boxer Rebellion, had just become the governor of Shansi. He lived in Taiyuan.

Also living in this capital city were a group of various missionaries dedicated to bringing the Gospel to the Shansi region. Dr. William Wilson operated a hospital for opium addicts at his own expense. He lived there with his wife and young son. Although he was already due for furlough, he had put it off because of the many victims of the famine that was ravaging the area. While he tirelessly worked on, he came down with peritonitis, an inflammation of the membrane in the abdomen cavity.

Just after the killings started, Wilson traveled twenty miles to help a Chinese doctor who had been slashed by a Boxer sword. Although very sick, Wilson made the trip and was able to help the wounded man. On the way there, he penned his last letter. "It's all fog," he wrote a fellow doctor, "but I think, old chap, that we are on the edge of a volcano, and I fear Taiyuan is the inner edge." He wouldn't live to know how true those words were.

With Mrs. Wilson were two China Inland Mission workers who were single. Jane Stevens, a nurse who was in frail health at the time, had arrived in China fifteen years prior in 1885. During her last trip to England there were those who attempted to persuade her to stay in England. She replied, "I don't feel I have yet finished the work God has for me in China. I must go back. Perhaps—who knows—I may be among those allowed to give their lives for the people."

Mildred Clarke, her fellow CIM missionary wrote, "I long to live a poured-out life unto Him among these Chinese, and to enter into the fellowship of His sufferings for souls, who poured out His life unto death for us."

Also operating in Taiyuan in 1900 was the Sheo Yang Mission, which operated a hospital for the people of the area. Part of this group were Thomas Pigott and his wife Jessie. One friend later wrote of him, "If ever a man lived in earnest, it was Thomas Wellesley Pigott." The Pigotts had been in China for years and had lost good friends in another massacre that had occurred five years previously. Since that time the Pigotts had felt that their time in China would be short and had worked feverishly to accomplish as much as possible while they had the chance.

It was late June when the trouble started. Boxer gangs roamed the streets, setting fire to the compounds of the Sheo Yang Mission and also of a British Baptist group. They all managed to escape those buildings and make it to the Baptist boys' school, about a half mile away. Edith Coombs, one of the Baptist missionaries, suddenly realized that they had left behind two Chinese schoolgirls in the compound. She ran back the half mile and into the burning building to rescue the girls. As they were rushing out, the one girl who was sick stumbled and fell. By this time the mob was converging on them, throwing rocks and bricks at them. She was forced back into the burning house where the last the young girls saw of her she was kneeling down in the flames.

For the next two weeks the remaining thirty-two missionaries stayed barricaded in the school building. Day and night stones were hurled at the door and walls, while the missionaries huddled inside, praying that the governor would rescue them. On July 9 soldiers showed up and escorted them all to the governor's courtyard. They were joined there by twelve Catholic priests. The dear people's hopes were dashed when the governor himself came out brandishing a sword and screaming, "Kill! Kill!"

He announced that the men would die first. George Farthing, one of the Baptists and a father of three, stepped forward. His wife tried to cling to him but he gently set her aside and knelt before the chopping block. One quick slash of the sword took his head. One by one the men were killed in like fashion. Then it was the women. Mrs. Farthing's children had to be pulled away from her, as she was forced to place her neck on the bloody block.

After the carnage was completed, their bodies were left out where they were stripped clean of clothes and valuables that evening. Their remains were placed in cages for all to see on the city wall.

WEEK 15: CHOICES

Monday   BIBLICAL EXAMPLES OF TEMPTATION

MEMORY VERSE: I CORINTHIANS 10:13

Everybody makes choices everyday. In fact, even animals must continually make decisions and choices. This is part of life. In this life, God has given us the right and ability to choose between right and wrong, sin and obedience, submission and rebellion. Our days are filled with opportunities to make proper decisions. The more we respond obediently to these choices, the more we allow the Spirit of God to fill us and control us.

In each of the following stories, tell what the temptation was, what choices were made, the outcome of those choices, and how you think you would have responded.

1. Genesis 13:8-18; 19:24-26

2. Joshua 7:20-26

3. II Kings 5:15-27

4. Job 2:7-10

5. Daniel 1:3-16

1. Read Matthew 4:1-11 and then I John 2:15-17. Compare Christ's three temptations to the three areas of temptation the Apostle John wrote of. Then, explain what three areas of temptation we face as believers in Christ.

2. Temptation comes to us through three primary sources: the world, the flesh, and the devil. Look up each of the following passages and tell which is spoken of and what you learn from it.

 a. Genesis 25:29-33

 b. I Kings 11:1-8

 c. I Chronicles 21:1-8

 d. Romans 6:12-16

 e. II Corinthians 11:3

 f. II Peter 2:18-22

1. Read Romans 13:14 and explain what you think it means.

2. People often set themselves up to fall into sin by placing themselves in situations that will lead them astray. In each of the passages that follow, explain what you see as the provision for sin and what you should do to guard yourself from falling into temptation.

    a. Proverbs 4:20-27

    b. Proverbs 7:6-27

    c. Proverbs 22:24-25

    d. I Corinthians 15:33

3. Think back to when you were continually falling into sin. List five things in your life that you feel made it easier for you to fall into sin.

1. Read the following verses and explain what you learn about resisting temptation.

    a. I Corinthians 10:13

    b. Hebrews 2:18

    c. James 1:2-4

2. List five consequences you may face if you fall back into your old lifestyle.

    1.

    2.

    3.

    4.

    5.

3. List five things you have to look forward to if you sustain victory in your life.

    1.

    2.

    3.

    4.

    5.

It is a spiritual truth that God tests the faith of His people—or allows it to be tested. He does this in a number of ways and for a number of reasons. In each of the following verses, explain the situation, how the person is being tested, and why you think the Lord is allowing it.

1. Genesis 22:1-2

2. Deuteronomy 8:2

3. I Kings 3:5-15

4. I Kings 17: 9-24

5. Job 2:1-10

6. Psalm 13:1-6

7. John 6:5-13

8. John 11:1-44

In the northwest part of China, a small group of Christian and Missionary Alliance missionaries carried on their work. When news of the Boxer Rebellion came to them, they attempted to flee to Mongolia on camels. Bandits intercepted them, however, and took everything they had, including their clothes. The experience was so traumatic that two of the women gave birth prematurely. They lived for two weeks in the desert, without clothes and eating roots to stay alive.

No sooner were they rescued by some Catholic priests, when news came that a Boxer army was approaching. "Our way... is cut off," the Alliance's Carl Lundberg wrote. "If we are not able to escape, tell our friends we live and die for the Lord. I do not regret coming to China. The Lord has called me and His grace is sufficient. The way He chooses is best for me. His will be done. Excuse my writing, my hand is shivering."[22]

A few days later they were all killed.

In Fenchow, a city of northern Shansi province, another group of missionaries were found by a local magistrate. He ordered them out of the city, under the pretense of protection by a group of armed guards. They were apparently expecting the worse. Lizzie Atwater wrote the following letter twelve days before they were all killed:

"Dear ones, I long for a sight of your dear faces, but I fear we shall not meet on earth... I am preparing for the end very quietly and calmly. The Lord is wonderfully near, and He will not fail me. I was very restless and excited while there seemed a chance of life, but God had taken away that feeling, and now I just pray for grace to meet the terrible end bravely. The pain will soon be over; and oh the sweetness of the welcome above!

"My little baby will go with me. I think God will give it to me in Heaven, and my dear mother will be so glad to see us. I cannot imagine the Savior's welcome. Oh, that will compensate for all these days of suspense. Dear ones, live near to God and cling less closely to earth. There is no other way by which we can receive that peace from God which passeth understanding... I must keep calm and still these hours. I do not regret coming to China, but am sorry I have done so little. My married life, two precious years, has been so very full of happiness. We will die together, my dear husband and I."[23]

Another group of missionaries were also soon to meet a similar fate. Annie King and Elizabeth Burton, both young, attractive women from Britain, had been in China less than two years when the trouble began. Annie wrote home, "It is so nice to be in this village, where the people trust us, and love to hear of Jesus, for whose sake and the Gospel's we have come. There are numbers of villages where the name of Jesus is unknown, all in heathen darkness, without a ray of light."[24]

Elizabeth wrote, "Oh, I feel so inadequate, so weak, and yet I hear Him say, 'Go in this thy might, have not I sent thee?' Yes, He has sent me; if ever I felt God has called me in my life, I feel it tonight." [25]

John and Sarah Young had been married only fifteen months. She had written in her application to China Inland Mission (CIM), "I want to be found in the battle when He comes, and I want to be an instrument in the hands of God in saving souls from death."[26]

Also with the four were George and Belle McConnell, who had just buried their daughter in Scotland two years before. As the group traveled on the road to Yu-men-k'ou, they were met by a band of soldiers who advised them to detour off the main road for safety's sake. They promised them protection but as soon as they got off the road they turned on them. "Our orders are to kill you unless you promise to stop preaching your foreign religion." When the missionaries refused to quit, they pulled Mr. McConnell from his mule and decapitated him. They then yanked his wife and young son to the ground. Kenneth, the young boy said, "Papa does not allow you to kill little Kennie." Both were killed instantly as were the others.

WEEK 16: BIBLICAL LOVE

Monday   OUR LOVE FOR GOD

MEMORY VERSE: MATTHEW 22:37-39

Read the following verses and tell what is promised to those who love the Lord.

1. Exodus 20:6

2. Deuteronomy 7:9

3. Psalm 37:4

4. Psalm 91:14

5. Psalm 145:20

6. Isaiah 56:6-7

7. Romans 8:28

1. Christians often try to win converts through words—through the intellect. Many mistakenly think that they can convince others through persuasive arguments why the Bible is true and why they should become Christians. What they don't realize is that if you can be convinced *to be* a Christian, you can be convinced *not to be* a Christian. People aren't won to true Christianity through persuasion; they are only won as they see Christ and His love in Christians' lives. Look up the following verses and tell what you learn about the importance of loving one another.

     a. John 13:34-35

     b. I Thessalonians 4:9-12

     c. James 1:27

     d. I Peter 3:1-4

     e. Colossians 3:14

     f. Ephesians 4:16

1. There is a great emphasis placed on signs, miracles, healings and tongues in Pentecostal circles. I Corinthians chapters 12 and 14 are expounded at length to show that these gifts are indeed for the Chrsitian Body today. Unfortunately, little is said about the chapter between the two that is the real basis for it all. Read I Corinthians 13:1-3. List those activities that can be done without love.

   1.   4.

   2.   5.

   3.   6.

2. Now look up Matthew 7:21-23 and list the things that can be done by those who are on their way to hell. Do you see any comparison?

   1.

   2.

   3.

3. Look up Romans 13:8-10 and answer the following questions.

   a. According to verse 8, what are you indebted to do?

   b. Look up the Greek word used for "debt" in the *Strong's* and the *Vine's* and give its definition.

   c. According to verse 10, what affect does love have on the law?

4. Write out I John 4:7-8

5. Write out I John 3:18

Turn again to I Corinthians 13. In verses 4-7 there are 14 different things that love does or does not do. Elaborate on what each one of these "love principles" means and then give an illustration out of your own life how you can do better in that area to those with whom you live and work.

1. Love is *patient.*

2. Love is *kind.*

3. Love is *not jealous.*

4. Love *does not brag* and is *not arrogant.*

5. Love *does not act unbecomingly.*

6. Love *does not seek its own.*

7. Love is *not provoked.*

8. Love *does not take into account a wrong suffered.*

9. Love *does not rejoice in unrighteousness but in the truth.*

10. Love *bears, believes, hopes and endures all things.* Love *never fails.*

1. Look up the following verses and tell what you learn about what love does and does not do.

   a. John 15:12-13

   b. Ephesians 4:2,15

   c. Proverbs 10:12

   d. I Corinthians 8:1

   e. I John 4:18

2. Look up the word "love" in the *Vine's* and tell what you learn about the two Greek verbs.

During the next fifty years after the Boxer Rebellion ended, bloodshed continued throughout China. Although the ending of the riots marked a time of great evangelization across the country, the same fears and prejudices were still to be found amongst many of the people. In 1931, President Chiang Kai-shek declared himself to be a Christian. This was, of course, a great victory in one sense but with it came renewed attacks upon Christians from Kai-shek's enemies: the communists. In Kiangsi Province alone, the communists killed an estimated one hundred and fifty thousand Chinese in 1930. There was great political tension in China during this time and the Christians were caught in the middle.

To make matters worse, the decade of the thirties began with terrible famines and plagues. Dissidents often blamed the missionary doctors (who were giving their lives to the Chinese people expecting nothing in return) for spreading plagues with their poison (medicine). It was often also said that the "gods" were angry with the people because of the Christians which was the reason for the droughts and famines.

In Minchow, a town of the Kansu Province, an Assemblies of God school located there lost one hundred and fifty students out of five hundred from the plague. Bandits then struck the town, torturing and killing people to force them to give up their valuables. Hundreds were burned or beaten, amongst whom were many Christians. No sooner did the bandits leave town than an army of thirty thousand Muslims took over the town and made their headquarters in the front yard of the Assemblies mission house. The Muslims were there for eighteen days, looting, burning, raping and killing people. When missionary W. W. Simpson attempted to have a worship service, one of the General's staff members arrogantly sat on the platform and made motions with his sword of cutting off the missionary's head. Simpson continued to preach about the coming of Christ into the world and for some reason the officer didn't kill him.

In October 1931, widower Jack Vinson was captured by bandits while visiting churches in Kiangsu Province. A government force pursued the bandits and surrounded them in a small town. The bandits offered Vinson his freedom if he would persuade the army to leave. Vinson agreed only if they released others also held. The bandits refused and tried to shoot their way out. In the commotion many of them were killed and the survivors fled with Vinson, but because of recent surgery he could not run and was shot and beheaded.

One witness of the account reported that the bandit told him, "I'm going to kill you. Aren't you afraid?" Vinson simply replied, "Kill me, if you wish. I will go straight to God." A fellow Southern Presbyterian minister, E.H. Hamilton, was inspired by his courage to write a poem that became the theme of all of the missionaries in China.

Afraid? Of What?

To feel the spirit's glad release?
To pass from pain to perfect peace,
The strife and strain of life to cease?
Afraid - of that?

Afraid? Of What?
Afraid to see the Savior's face,
To hear His welcome, and to trace
The glory gleam from wounds of grace?
Afraid - of that?

Afraid? Of What?
A flash, a crash, a pierced heart;
Darkness, light, O Heaven's art!
A wound of His a counterpart!
Afraid - of that?

Afraid? Of What?
To do by death what life could not -
Baptize with blood a stony plot,
Till souls shall blossom from the spot?
Afraid - of that?

WEEK 17: BIBLICAL FORGIVENESS

Monday   OUR NEED FOR FORGIVENESS

MEMORY VERSE: COLOSSIANS 3:12-13

Forgiveness is key in the Scriptures. Man's greatest need is for forgiveness. Without it, we have no hope for a relationship with God, no hope for the atoning work of Calvary, no hope for eternity. The reason man needs forgiveness is because of his fallen nature. When Adam fell into sin in the Garden of Eden, we all fell into sin. Paul said, *"...through one man sin entered into the world, and death through sin, and so death spread to all men, because all sinned".* (Rom. 5:12) Man's nature has become perverse and depraved and "the depravity of man" has become one of the foundations of doctrine of every major denomination.

Look up the following verses supporting the doctrine of "the depravity of man" and tell what you learn about it.

1. Jeremiah 17:9

2. Psalm 51:5

3. Psalm 14:3

4. Proverbs 22:15

5. I John 1:8

In the second chapter of *At the Altar of Sexual Idolatry,* I spoke of how an ungrateful attitude toward God often leads a person into *dissatisfaction.* People don't appreciate their own forgiveness because they don't see the wickedness in their own lives. When that happens, they are usually overwhelmed with godly sorrow over their sinful condition. This is where true repentance begins.

What happens more often is that a person *intellectually* sees that he is sinful, *intellectually* confesses his need of a Savior and *intellectually* gives his life to Christ. Without getting into the salvation question, we can see that until a person really sees the reality of how he has lived in open defiance of God, how he has continually offended God with his belligerent attitudes and actions, and how God has been so gracious and long-suffering with him, he will tend not to appreciate God's forgiveness.

Most of us are much more prone to think, 1) that we aren't all that bad, 2) that we haven't done anything to offend God, and 3) that He owes it to us to forgive us. These attitudes contribute to a thankless and ungrateful heart toward God.

In today's homework, I would like you to prayerfully consider what you have done to sin against God. Make a list of sinful attitudes, habits and actions that you have done or had in the past. Before starting, ask God to show you the magnitude of these. If you put your heart into this, you might find that God will really move in your life.

If a person doesn't appreciate how much he has been forgiven of, he will not have any motivation to forgive others. What is incredible is how Christians—who have been forgiven for a lifetime of terrible crimes against God—can turn around and be so unmerciful toward those who do the slightest wrong to them.

1. Write out the last phrase of I Corinthians 13:5.

2. What does Paul say in Ephesians 4:32 is the basis for forgiving others?

3. Read the story Jesus told about forgiveness, found in Matthew 18:21-35, and answer the following questions.

   a. According to verse 22, how many times should we forgive those who wrong us?

   b. Realistically, how many times does it take for a brother to sin against you, for you to start building a case against him in your mind?

   c. Can you see your salvation experience in verses 26 & 27? How?

d. How many times have you acted like the servant in verses 28 through 30? Briefly tell about any instances that come to your mind about this.

e. Can you see the difference in the amounts owed as shown in verses 24 & 28?

f. Can you see the correlation to how much God has forgiven you?

g. Write out verses 34 & 35.

1. Look up the following verses and tell what you learn about forgiveness.

    a. Exodus 23:4-5:

    b. Proverbs 25:21-22:

    c. Matthew 6:12-15:

    d. Romans 12:14, 17-21:

    e. Colossians 3:13:

2. Read Psalm 103:8-14 and explain in your own words the kind of attitude you should have toward those who have offended you.

1. The first rule of living with a forgiving spirit is to walk in the Spirit, so that you are not easily provoked. I often have found that the more self-centered a person is, the "touchier" or more sensitive he tends to be. As we allow Christ to live through us, we are not offended as easily. Write out the following verses.

    a. Proverbs 19:11

    b. Ecclesiastes 7:21

    c. I Peter 4:8

2. Sometimes when someone hurts us, try as we might, we find it very difficult to forget what that person has done to us. Jesus was the Great Peacemaker. He was always interested in seeing man reconciled to God and reconciled to each other. Read Luke 6:27-28 and list the three things He says we can do that will help us to love and forgive those who have wronged us. If you will do these things *regularly*, you will find your feelings change toward that person!

    1.

    2.

    3.

3. When a Christian does something to offend us, we must—in love—think about what will benefit *them*. We do this for *their sake*, not as an excuse to get back at them! This takes real *agape* love. Read Luke 17:3-10 and answer the following questions.

    a. According to verse 3, what should we do if a "brother" (Christian) sins against us?

b. Read Galatians 6:1-3. Explain about the attitude you should take with you when confronting your brother.

c. In verse 5 we find the apostles were so overwhelmed by the idea of this that one of them blurted out, "Increase our faith!" What he was trying to say here was that he couldn't possibly handle a situation like this without the Lord's intervention. Jesus immediately rebuked that notion by telling them that faith like a mustard seed can uproot trees. More faith isn't what is required, but simple obedience. With that in mind, explain what you think the point of the story is in verses 7 through 10.

John and Betty Stam met at Moody Bible Institute not long after Jack Vinson's death. Challenged by God through the poem *Afraid? Of What?,* John responded to a call by China Inland Mission (CIM) for single men to serve in a dangerous, communist-infested area of China. Chosen to give the Class Address for the Moody Class of 1932, he told the student body,

"Shall we beat a retreat, and turn back from our high calling in Christ Jesus; or dare we advance at God's command in face of the impossible?... Let us remind ourselves that the Great Commission was never qualified by clauses calling for advance only if funds were plentiful and no hardship or self-denial involved. On the contrary, we are told to expect tribulation and even persecution, but with it victory in Christ."[27]

Since Betty had graduated from college a year prior to John, she had already gone over to begin her duty. Upon arriving in China, she was delayed from going to her assigned place as the missionary there, H. S. Ferguson, had been captured by bandits and was never seen alive again. John showed up a year later and in September 1934, they were blessed with a baby girl.

Assigned to Anhwei Province, they went to the town of Ching-te where the district magistrate assured them that he would protect them. A few weeks later communists attacked the town, and the magistrate was the first to flee! The communists went directly to where the Stams were living. Betty served them tea and cake while John tried to assure them that they had only peaceful intentions. When they finished their tea, the leader simply said, "You will go with us."

John was forced to write CIM a letter asking for a $20,000 ransom. He added in the letter, "The Lord bless and guide you, and as for us, may God be glorified whether by life or death." He later told his captors that he did not expect the ransom to be paid.

The "reds" withdrew from the town taking the Stams with them. Along the way they discussed killing the baby girl to save trouble. An old farmer who happened to be standing there protested and was told, "Then you will die for her." The farmer replied, "I am willing," and was killed instantly. John

was taken to the postmaster and ordered to write another ransom note. The man asked him where they were going. John replied, "We don't know where they're going, but we are going to heaven."

A little later they were stripped down to their underwear and painfully bound with rope. After a sleepless night they were marched through the town as the communists ridiculed them. All the townspeople were led out to watch the execution. Suddenly the town physician, a Christian by the name of Dr. Wang, ran up and pleaded with their captors to release them. He was led away to be killed. As John himself sought mercy for the doctor's life, he was ordered to kneel. The bandit flashed his sword and took off his head. Betty quivered and dropped, and the same befell her.

Somehow during the excitement of it all, the baby girl was found alive in a house by a Chinese evangelist who had just arrived. At great risk to himself and his family, he took the baby home and buried the bodies. The townspeople were moved by it all and gathered to hear the funeral sermon. The evangelist fearlessly preached Christ, and told the people that they too must repent.

After the funeral, the evangelist and his wife carried the baby hundreds of miles in a rice basket to the home of another missionary. This missionary took the baby to Betty Stam's parents, Dr. and Mrs. Charles Scott, who were also missionaries to China. Upon hearing of his daughter and son-in-law's death, Dr. Scott said, "They have not died in vain. The book of the martyrs is still the seed of the Church. If we could hear our beloved children speak, we know from their convictions that they would praise God because He counted them worthy to suffer for the sake of Christ."[28]

The report of their martyrdom and survival of the "miracle baby" was widely publicized in the United States. Hundred of letters came in to the Scotts. Many volunteered to take their places on the mission field. Students back at Moody began holding student prayer meetings for missionaries. A CIM missionary wrote Betty's parents, "A life which had the longest span of years might not have been able to do one-hundredth of the work for Christ which they have done in a day."[29]

WEEK 18: HIS WONDERFUL WORD

Monday   THE ETERNAL WORD

MEMORY VERSE: II TIMOTHY 3:16-17

1. Look up the following verses and tell what you learn about the Word of God.

    a. Psalms 119:89

    b. Isaiah 40:8

    c. Matthew 5:18

    d. Matthew 24:35

    e. I Peter 1:25

2. As a contrast, write out the following verses about man.

    a. Psalm 103:14-15

    b. Isaiah 40:7-8

    c. Romans 3:4

Look up the following verses and tell for each what you learn about the influence God's Word has on people's lives.

1. Isaiah 55:11

2. Jeremiah 5:14

3. Jeremiah 23:29

4. Romans 1:16

5. Ephesians 6:17

6. Hebrews 4:12

1. Read the following verses and tell about the consequences of rejecting the Word of God.

   a. II Chronicles 36:16

   b. Isaiah 5:24

   c. Hosea 4:6

   d. Amos 2:4

   e. Zechariah 7:12

2. Read Proverbs 1:20-33 and answer the following questions.

   a. According to verse 23, what must we do to have the Spirit poured out on us and His Words known to us?

   b. In verses 24 & 25, list the four responses given to the wisdom offered by God.

      1.   3.

      2.   4.

   c. In verses 26 & 27, list the four things that will come on the person who refuses God's wisdom.

      1.   3.

      2.   4.

Write out only the promises found in the following verses to those who treasure God's Word.

1. Psalm 119:9

2. Psalm 119:45

3. Psalm 119:133

4. Proverbs 2:1, 16

5. Proverbs 6:23-24

6. John 8:31-32

7. John 17:17

8. I Peter 1:22

Read Psalm 119. Pick out ten of your favorite verses about the Word. For each one, list the reference and say a few words about what it means to you personally.

1.

2.

3.

4.

5.

6.

7.

8.

9.

10.

Called the Dark Continent in the nineteenth century because Americans and Europeans knew so little about Africa, this second largest continent on planet earth was also known among missionary societies as "the white man's graveyard," because the average life expectancy of a missionary was only eight years. "Our God bids us first build a cemetery before we build a church or dwelling-house," wrote an early missionary, "showing us that the resurrection of... Africa must be effected by our own destruction."

Faithful unto Death

Twenty missionaries died at the London Missionary Society's central African station before the twentieth convert was baptized. A book published in 1902 listed 190 martyrs from ten North American missionary societies who succumbed to disease since 1833. A sampling from the Missionary Society of the Protestant Episcopal Church reveals the life span of fourteen missionaries.

Miss Isabella Alley - 1 year
Rev. J.C. Auer - 21 years
Miss Phebe Bart - 4 months
Miss Marha D. Coggeshall - 3 months
Mrs. C.C. Hoffman - 3 years
Rev. C.C. Hoffman - 16 years
Rev. H. H. Holcomb - 1 year
Rev. G.W. Horne - 2 years
Rev. E.J.P. Messenger - 3 months
Rev. Launcelot B. Minor - 7 years
Mrs. Catherine L. Parch - 2 years
Mrs. Jacob Rambo - 2 years
Rev. Robert Smith - 3 months
Dr. T.R. Steele - 6 months

Nothing deterred the early pioneers of the gospel. Wrote Willis R. Hotchkiss: "I have dwelt four years practically alone in Africa. I have been thirty times stricken with the fever, three times attacked by lions, and several times by rhinoceri; but let me say to you, I would gladly go through the whole thing again, if I could have the joy of again bringing the word "Savior" and flashing it into the darkness that envelops another tribe in central Africa."[30]

WEEK 19: PRAYER

Monday   SEEKING THE LORD

MEMORY VERSE: EPHESIANS 6:18-19

Look up the following verses and tell what you learn about seeking the Lord.

1. Psalm 9:10

2. Psalm 14:2

3. Isaiah 55:6

4. Jeremiah 29:13

5. Daniel 9:3

6. Hosea 10:12

7. Luke 11:9

8. Hebrews 11:6

1. Look up the following verses. In a word or two, tell what the cause of unanswered prayer is.

    a. Deuteronomy 1:45

    b. I Samuel 14:37

    c. I Samuel 28:6

    d. Psalm 66:18

    e. Proverbs 1:28

    f. Proverbs 21:13

    g. Proverbs 28:9

    h. Isaiah 1:15

    i. Isaiah 59:2

    j. Isaiah 64:7

    k. Hosea 5:6

    l. Micah 3:4

    m. Zechariah 7:13

    n. James 1:6-7

    o. James 4:3

2. Explain what you see as the main hindrance to your prayers being answered.

Look up the following verses and tell what you learn about successful prayer.

1. II Chronicles 7:14

2. Jeremiah 29:13

3. Matthew 6:5-6

4. Mark 11:24

5. John 14:13-14

6. James 5:16

7. I John 3:22

8. I John 5:14-15

1. Look up the following examples of those who wouldn't be denied in prayer. *Briefly* tell each story in your own words.

    a. Genesis 18:16-33

    b. Genesis 32:24-30

    c. Deuteronomy 9:18-19

    d. Matthew 15:22-28

    e. Acts 12:3-17

2. In each of the prior stories, there are two common denominators. Write what you think they are:

    1.

    2.

3. Read the story Jesus tells in Luke 18:1-8. Write out verse 5.

4. Write out I John 5:14-15. Tell why you think God "allows Himself to be convinced".

For each section of the Lord's Prayer given (Matthew 6:9-13), write out a personalized version for your own life.

1. *Our Father who is in heaven, Hallowed be Your name.*

2. *Your kingdom come,*

3. *Your will be done, on earth as it is in heaven.*

4. *Give us this day our daily bread.*

5. *And forgive us our debts, as we also have forgiven our debtors.*

6. *And do not lead us not into temptation, but deliver us from evil.*

7. *For Yours is the kingdom, and the power, and the glory forever. Amen.*

In the early sixties, six WEC missionaries ran a station in a dangerous area of the Congo. The sunbeam of the group was a young bachelor named Bill McChesney or "Smiling Bill," as everyone called him. Although only five foot two and a hundred and ten pounds, he made up for it with his exuberance. Shortly before leaving the states for the Congo, he wrote a poem which expressed his commitment:

My Choice

I want my breakfast served at eight, with ham and
 eggs upon the plate;
A well-broiled steak I'll eat at one, and dine again
 when day is done.
I want an ultramodern home and in each room a
 telephone;
Soft carpets, too, upon the floors, and pretty drapes
 to grace the doors.
A cozy place of lovely things, like easy chairs with
 inner springs,
And then I'll get a small TV—of course, "I'm care-
 ful what I see."
I want my wardrobe, too, to be of neatest, finest
 quality,
With latest style in suit and vest: Why should not
 Christians have the best?
But then the Master I can hear in no uncertain voice,
 so clear:
"I bid you come and follow Me, the lowly Man of
 Galilee."
"Birds of the air have made their nest, and foxes in
 their holes find rest,
But I can offer you no bed; no place have I to lay My
 head."
In shame I hung my head and cried. How could I
 spurn the Crucified?
Could I forget the way He went, the sleepless nights
 in prayer He spent?
For forty days without a bite, alone He fasted day
 and night;
Despised, rejected—on He went, and did not stop
 till veil He rent.
A man of sorrows and of grief, no earthly friend to
 bring relief;
"Smitten of God," the prophet said—Mocked,
 beaten, bruised, His blood ran red.

If He be God, and died for me, no sacrifice too great
 can be
For me, a mortal man, to make; I'll do it all for Jesus'
 sake.
Yes, I will tread the path He trod, no other way will
 please my God;
So, henceforth, this my choice shall be, my choice
 for all eternity."[31]

The Congo during this time was tense with strife. The Simbas, a tribe rebellious to the white rule in Africa, was attacking and killing people all around the area. They repeatedly put the missionaries at the little compound through terrifying trial runs of coming to kill them; only to leave without harm.

On November 14, 1964 they came and took little Bill McChesney away; even though he was ill with malaria. Also being held captive were four missionaries from another compound. One of them, James Rodger was the opposite to the effervescent "Smiling Bill" in every way. Though solemn and staid, his love for the Lord was unquestionable. During their ten days together there the two became dear friends.

One day an arriving rebel officer turned livid when he saw Bill McChesney. "Why is this man still free?" he demanded. "Take him to prison at once!" When Bill was pushed into a truck, Jim Rodger jumped in to accompany his new friend. During the trip, the soldiers beat Bill mercilessly. Weakened by the malaria, the little guy couldn't stand under the attack and upon arriving, Jim had to carry him into the prison.

The next morning a colonel arrived and demanded to know their nationalities. Bill acknowledged being American, Jim British. Upon hearing this the colonel was about to have just Bill killed but Jim stood next to him saying, "If you must die, brother, I'll die with you."

The colonel motioned for the mob of rebels to attack them. They came at them swinging clubs and fists. Bill was killed quickly. Jim caught him and gently laid him on the ground. The mob then knocked him down and kicked and trampled him to death also.

WEEK 20: SPIRITUAL WARFARE

Monday   ENEMY TERRITORY

MEMORY VERSE: REVELATION 12:10-11

1. We have been called "citizens of heaven." The world is our battlefield, not our home. We have been called to be soldiers in this warfare. Write out II Timothy 2:3-4 and explain in your own words what you think this passage of Scripture is saying to *you*.

2. If we *are* in the enemy's territory and if we *are* in a war, then we should expect to live with a "warfare mentality." We should expect to be assaulted and occasionally hurt in this battle. Look up the following verses and relate them to this battle we are in.

   a. Matthew 5:10-12

   b. Romans 8:17

   c. I Peter 4:12-14

   .   d. Revelation 13:7

3. Read Jesus' account of what it will be like in the last days found in Matthew 10:16-39. Describe how you can see spiritual victory in this kind of lifestyle (which one day you very likely will have to live).

1. Look up the following verses and tell what you learn about how Satan and his fallen angels operate.

    a. Job 2:7

    b. Zechariah 3:1

    c. Matthew 4:1

    d. Matthew 13:19, 38-39

    e. John 8:44

    f. II Corinthians 2:11

    g. II Corinthians 11:3

    h. II Thessalonians 2:9

2. Can you see through this that he is limited in what he can do to you? Can you see that you are in the hands of God and that, if you stay there, you have nothing to fear from Satan?

1. Write out II Corinthians 10:3-5. Describe what kind of "lofty" things there are in your heart that Satan could use to hinder you from coming into a heartfelt knowledge of God.

2. Look up the following verses. Tell what the weapons are and how they can be used.

   a. Romans 13:12

   b. II Corinthians 6:7

   c. Ephesians 6:14-17

   d. I Thessalonians 5:8

   e. Hebrews 4:12

Our victory in warfare depends upon God. The battle is His. Our responsibility is only to stay obediently in His will. As long as we do that, our victory is assured because it is God who fights our battles. Look up the following verses and tell what you learn about this.

1. Exodus 14:14

2. Exodus 23:27

3. II Chronicles 16:9

4. II Chronicles 32:8

5. Psalm 34:7

6. Psalm 44:5

7. Psalm 91:4

8. Luke 10:19

Satan operates in the temporal realm. He tries to make us see everything in a temporal setting. He knows that if he can get our eyes off the Lord and onto our troubles, he has succeeded in blinding us. He will attack, hinder our efforts, tempt us into ungodly behavior, attempt to frighten us and deceive us. But as we saw in yesterday's study, we are in the hands of the Almighty. Satan can do no more to us than either,

    (1) we allow him to do through our willful disobedience to God, or

    (2) God allows him to do for the purpose of strengthening our faith.

We have been purchased with the blood of the Lamb; we are no longer Satan's possession. What we must keep in mind, however, is that we live in the eternal realm and that is where our victory is assured. Look up the following verses and tell what you learn about the victory that we are assured of.

1. John 16:33

2. Romans 8:35-37

3. Ephesians 1:3-5

4. Ephesians 2:1-7

5. I John 5:4

6. Revelation 2:7

7. Revelation 3:5

8. Revelation 3:21

9. Revelation 21:7

Life in Europe in the 1920s and early 1930s was very simple for most folks; especially so for a simple Dutch family who operated a watch repair shop in Haarlem. All of Europe watched Germany with suspicion as Adolf Hitler came to power. When he began his march on various countries, the others knew it would be only a matter of time before theirs too would fall. In 1939 the inevitable German *blitzkrieg* came. The small Dutch army fell within five days.

At first, occupation wasn't so bad. Gradually though, the grip of the German forces grew tighter and tighter. Rules became stricter, rations smaller, curfew earlier. The Ten Boom family calmly went about their normal routine as most other Dutch families did. It all began to change when the Germans started arresting and harassing Jewish families. These simple folks loved their Lord and couldn't just shut out the need of those who were hurting.

What began as simply trying to help some Jews out gradually grew into a full-blown "underground railroad" for getting Jewish people to safety. To do this was no simple matter. Corrie, who had inadvertently become the leader of the work, had to have contacts with underground workers from around the country. She needed ration cards, food and places to send the hunted people.

And then there was the matter of what to do with those Jews who nobody would take for various reasons. The Ten Booms couldn't just send them away, so they had a secret room built into the house for the people to hide in if the dreaded Gestapo raid ever happened. And one night it finally did. There was a pounding at the door and in rushed the Gestapo.

The seven Jews managed to make it into the secret *Hiding Place* without getting caught. But the Germans had enough evidence to know that the Ten Booms were involved with the underground. Corrie, her sister Betsie, their father and several others were all hauled off to a prison. As time went on the inmates could hear the rumble of war getting closer and closer. One night they were all rousted out of their beds and told they were to evacuate. The inmates could hardly contain their excitement as they anticipated freedom. But their hopes were soon crushed as they were loaded onto trains and taken farther away from the war front.

Late the next night they arrived at a prison camp named Vught. Life was hard but at least Corrie and Betsie were together. They soon settled into a boring, predictable routine of working on aircraft instruments. The Germans made them work eleven hours a day and fed them only a piece of hard bread in the morning and a bowl of colored liquid for supper. The camp at Vught was split between male and female prisoners. Many of Betsie and Corrie's fellow inmates had husbands in the other side of the prison. These poor women were in a constant state of worry over their husbands.

Soon the warfront again caught up with them. As it did, the guards became more and more brutal. Inmates who were late for roll call or had any other problem were beaten mercilessly. Then the firing squads began in the men's prison. Every day the shootings increased.

Then again, they were all suddenly rounded up for another move. The women were herded into box cars so tightly they couldn't sit and taken on a trip that lasted several days. Deep into Germany they had gone. The women weren't given any food or water and weren't allowed to use a bathroom during this whole trip.

Finally the train came grinding to a stop. As the weakened pack of women fell out of the car, they were again herded into marching formation. After a walk through a small town they finally came to the pale gray walls of a place they had only heard horrible rumors about: Ravensbruck concentration camp.

Life here was more horrible than either of them could have dreamed in their worst nightmare. Corrie tells about it in her own words:

"Morning roll call at Ravensbruck came half an hour earlier than at Vught. By 4:30 A.M. we had to be standing outside in the black predawn chill, standing at parade attention in blocks of one hundred women, ten wide, ten deep. Sometimes after hours of this we would gain the shelter of the barracks only to hear the whistle.

"'Everybody out! Fall in for roll call!'

"Barracks 8 was in the quarantine compound. Next to us—perhaps as a deliberate warning to newcomers—were located the punishment barracks. From there, all day long and often into the night, came the sounds of hell itself. They were not the sounds of anger, or of any human emotion, but of a cruelty altogether detached: blows landing in regular rhythm, screams keeping pace. We would stand in our ten-deep ranks with our hands trembling at our sides, longing to jam them against our ears, to make the sounds stop.

"The instant of dismissal we would mob the door of Barracks 8, stepping on each other's heels in our eagerness to get inside, to shrink the world back to understandable proportions.

"It grew harder and harder. Even within these four walls there was too much misery, too much seemingly pointless suffering. Every day something else failed to make sense, something else grew too heavy. 'Will You carry this too, Lord Jesus?'

"But as the rest of the world grew stranger, one thing became increasingly clear. And that was the reason the two of us were here. Why others should suffer we were not shown. As for us, from morning until lights-out, whenever we were not in ranks for roll call, our Bible was the center of an ever-widening circle of help and hope. Like waifs clustered around a blazing fire, we gathered about it, holding out our hearts to its warmth and light. The blacker the night around us grew, the brighter and truer and more beautiful burned the word of God. 'Who shall separate us from the love of Christ? Shall tribulation, or distress, or persecution, or famine, or nakedness, or peril, or sword?... Nay, in all these things we are more than conquerors through him that loved us.'

"I would look about us as Betsie read, watching the light leap from face to face. More than conquerors .... It was not a wish. It was a fact. We knew it, we experienced it minute by minute—poor, hated, hungry. We are more than conquerors. Not 'we shall be.' We are! Life in Ravensbruck took place on two separate levels, mutually impossible. One, the observable, external life, grew every day more horrible. The other, the life we lived with God, grew daily better, truth upon truth, glory upon glory.

"Sometimes I would slip the Bible from its little sack with hands that shook, so mysterious had it become to me. It was new; it had just been written. I marveled sometimes that the ink was dry. I had believed the Bible always, but reading it now had nothing to do with belief. It was simply a description of the way things were—of hell and heaven, of how men act and how God acts. I had read a thousand times the story of Jesus' arrest—how soldiers had slapped Him, laughed at Him, flogged Him. Now such happenings had faces and voices."[32]

And such was life for these two dear saints in Ravensbruck concentration camp. Before long, Betsie's feeble body began deteriorating; she had to be taken into the "hospital." To Corrie's utter horror, Betsie died. But God is good. It wasn't but a couple of weeks later that, through a clerical error, Corrie was released and sent back to Holland. For forty years after Ravensbruck, Corrie Ten Boom told the marvelous story of how God's presence could even be found in a hell on earth.

WEEK 21: THE POWER OF MEEKNESS

Monday   SUBMISSION TO GOD

MEMORY VERSE: MATTHEW 11:28-30

We live in a world where the strong survive and the weak are brushed aside. There is great competitiveness–especially in America. People striving with each other desperately trying to be first, get what they want, be recognized as the best. Competitive sports have become the national pastime. We root for our team to win.

What would happen if a group of people entered this fray on a different agenda? What would happen if this group of people showed great joy and peace while....losing? What would happen if these people refused to compete? What would happen if they began putting others first, letting others win? This is the great call of Christianity. This is the foundation of Christianity. To want to be a Christian, but not be willing to be this way, is absolutely contradictory.

Meekness begins in submission to God. This is found in two basic ways: (1) Living obediently to the commands He has given us through His Word, and (2) Living daily in submission to His will for our lives. The first refers to a general, overall lifestyle of obedience. The second refers to staying submitted to the specific direction He has for our own lives.

Many mistakenly think the first is all that is required. The thinking goes something like this: "I am to live a good life, pay my tithes, go to church, etc. But I decide what I want to do with my life. I decide where to go to church. I decide how many kids to have, etc." The notion comes from the idea that God gave us a brain and we should use it for ourselves. This is nothing more than an excuse for those who don't wish to submit to God's will for their lives.

Look up the following verses about His will, and tell what you learn from each.

1. Matthew 7:21

2. Matthew 12:50

3. Matthew 26:39, 42

4. John 7:17

5. Ephesians 6:6

1. Write out I Corinthians 6:20 and explain what this means to your life.

2. Look up the following verses about servanthood. Explain what you learn about it from each.

   a. Deuteronomy 28:47-48

   b. Psalm 116:16

   c. Matthew 20:25-28

   d. Luke 16:13

   e. John 12:26

   f. Galatians 5:13

3. Spend a few minutes and think about what it means to be a *servant of Christ*. Here are some things to think about: If I were someone's servant...
   • Could I do what I wanted to do when I wanted?
   • Could I have a life of my own?
   • Could I marry who I wanted to marry?
   • What could I expect if I were rebellious or disobedient?
   • Would I really find contentment in trying to resist my master's will?

   Now put all of this into perspective of being a servant (or slave) of Christ. Describe in practical terms how your life should be affected.

1. Look up the following verses. For each, write one word which describes the rights Christ gave up for you.

    a. Matthew 20:28

    b. John 5:30

    c. John 10:11

    d. II Corinthians 8:9

2. Read John 15:20.

    a. Describe the price Jesus paid.

    b. Explain the principle involved here in view of what we are studying.

3. Make a list of the ten most important rights you feel are yours as a human being. (Examples: "I have a right to be treated fairly. I have a right to a raise at work because I work the hardest. I have a right to dinner on time. I have a right not to be stuck in traffic.")

    1.

    2.

    3.

    4.

    5.

    6.

    7.

    8.

    9.

    10.

4. Read Philippians 2:1-8 and examine your attitude about your rights in view of the attitude Jesus exemplified. If you then feel a need to, go down your list of rights and give them one by one to the Lord.

When two people have a decision to make that they disagree upon, or have a run-in over some matter, someone's will must prevail. Sometimes they can compromise or work things out to fit both of their desires, but there will always be the issue of who is going to get more of their own way.

Those who strive attempt to handle these situations by overcoming the other person's will. Often people who do this don't even realize they are being selfish. To them it is simply a problem that they must solve by convincing the other person to do things *their* way. The way they think to accomplish this is to *overcome* the other's objections, arguments or—will.

What Jesus taught us was to *overcome*—not the self-centered desires of others—but those of *ourselves*. He didn't teach us to *overcome* others but to *go under* others. This is meekness—the willingness to allow others to have *their* way. Look up the following verses. Tell for each what you learn about "going under" the will of another.

1. Proverbs 15:1

2. Proverbs 15:18

3. Proverbs 17:14

4. Matthew 5:38-42

5. Romans 12:10

6. I Peter 3:8-9

Moses was called by God the *meekest* man on earth. Time and time again, when the people under him would raise up in rebellion to his authority, he would humbly plead with them to submit to God. He never tried to overcome them through the strength of his own personality or might. In fact, on more than one occasion, Moses pleaded with God not to destroy them. Because of his lowliness, Moses was allowed an intimacy with God that no other person has ever had. It is lowliness which brings us into the presence of God. It is the basis for the power of God to be poured out through us to others.

Pray through the following five verses. Describe for each one what the Lord shows you about coming close to Him.

1. Psalm 34:18

2. Psalm 51:17

3. Isaiah 57:15

4. Isaiah 66:2

5. I Peter 5:5-6

Born to a prominent German family in 1906, Deitrich Bonhoeffer entered seminary upon finishing college. What he found there was a dry and cynical formalism. Although only a student, he opposed the liberal teachings of some of his professors. He contended that the essential nature of the church should be viewed through the gospel of Jesus Christ, not through sociological reasoning.

In 1933 the Nazis overtook the parliament. This same year, the German Lutheran bishops issued a statement that said in part, "We German Protestant Christians accept the saving of our nation by our leader Adolf Hitler as a gift from God's hand."

On January 31 of that year, young Deitrich spoke over Berlin radio on the "concept of leadership." He pointedly asked Germans to consider their perceived need of a strong leader. He also asked them to consider when leadership is healthy, and when is it pathological and extreme. The message was cut off the air halfway through it.

Four weeks later communists burned the Reichstag building, which gave Hitler the excuse he needed to restrict free speech, free press and a number of other liberties. A couple of months after this Hitler began his systematic terrorization against German Jews.

Hitler attempted to exercise control over the Lutheran church by appointing one of his stooges in leadership over the entire denomination. Bonhoeffer and a group of reformers who called themselves the "Confessing Church" refused to go along with the bishops who aligned themselves with Hitler. The church split.

In the fall of 1934 the first arrests of Confessing Church ministers began. Little by little the Nazis began tightening their grip on the country and on the church. In 1937, Hitler's minister of church affairs, Hans Kerrl, gave a speech wherein he said that belief in Christ as the Son of God was "laughable." As Nazism rose, the real church went further underground.

In March 1939, Bonhoeffer went to New York to attempt to warn Lutheran leaders of the serious situation in Germany. While there, he was offered a position to minister to German refugees. He was tempted to stay but his conscience called him back to his own people. Not long after returning, his activities were restricted by the Gestapo. Leaders in the resistance got the order rescinded and got him a job in the counterespionage department known as the Abwehr. This was a wonderful cover for his real work which was to warn Christians outside the country of what Hitler was doing.

Bonhoeffer was eventually asked to participate in a conspiracy to have Hitler assassinated. He struggled with this question for months and finally agreed to help. The attempt was unsuccessful and in April of 1943 he was arrested.

For two years young Deitrich was held in German prisons. Three weeks before the double suicide of Hitler and Eva Braun, Bonhoeffer was taken with some other inmates into a forest outside their prison. They were ordered to strip and subsequently shot.

Probably the most profound legacy he left behind was his book entitled *The Cost of Discipleship*. In this heavily challenging work Bonhoeffer called on Christians to repent of "cheap grace" that has no cost and no substance. The man who paid the ultimate price for his Christian witness pleaded with others not to delude themselves into thinking they were saved when they weren't. He said:

"Cheap grace is the preaching of forgiveness without requiring repentance, baptism without church discipline, Communion without confession, absolution without personal confession. Cheap grace is grace without discipleship, grace without the cross, grace without Jesus Christ, living and incarnate ....

"Costly grace is the gospel which must be sought again and again, the gift which must be *asked* for, the door at which a man must *knock*.

"Such grace is *costly* because it calls us to follow, and it is *grace* because it calls us to follow *Jesus Christ*. It is costly because it costs a man his life, and it is grace because it gives a man the only true life. It is costly because it condemns sin, and grace because it justifies the sinner. Above all, it is *costly* because it cost God the life of His Son ...."[33]

WEEK 22: SIMPLE LIVING

Monday   LIVING LIKE KINGS IN SATAN'S KINGDOM

MEMORY VERSE: LUKE 16:13

"In proportion as our mind is brought into agreement with God's mind, so do we discover that the true life is after all the simple life—the life of one aim, of one path—of one controlling passion. The aim is the glory of God. The path is the will of God. And the passion is the love of God."

- W. H. Griffith Thomas

I recently heard two different statistics that I believe say a great deal about our struggles with sexual sin. The first said that the living standard of the average welfare recipient in America ranks within the average living standard of the top ten countries in the world. What that means is that the poor in America are actually better off than the middle-class people of over two hundred and forty other nations. The second statistic states that the average American cat eats better than at least one billion people on our planet.

We in America enjoy a standard of living that truly has more opulence, luxury, pleasure and comfort than any king has ever enjoyed in the history of the world. No king of the past has ever enjoyed indoor plumbing, electricity, television, newspapers, toasters, automobiles, ambulance service, telephones and all of the other things that many now consider necessities in life.

We live like kings but often forget that God's kingdom isn't of this world. This is the kingdom of Satan and its allurements are *his* rewards. We have become accustomed to such a high standard of living that we have allowed ourselves to become convinced that *we must sustain it*. We have allowed the things of this world to dominate our hearts. Since the flesh has been so pampered and catered to—it demands sexual sin and we have no power to deny its passions. Our lives are ruled by the lusts of the flesh.

Look up the following verses about materialism and wealth. Explain what you learn from them. (Keep in mind that *you* are *rich*).

1. Proverbs 18:11, 23

2. Ezekiel 28:5

3. Matthew 19:24

4. Luke 6:24-25

5. James 5:5

1. In Matthew 13 we find the parable of the "Sower and the Seed."

    a. Look up verse 22 and describe what wealth does to a person's walk with the Lord.

    b. Can you see any of its effects in your own life?

2. Look up I Timothy 6:9-11 and answer the following questions.

    a. In verse 9, list the four things those who want to get rich fall into.

       1.   3.

       2.   4.

    b. According to verse 9, what is the outcome of falling into these four things?

    c. According to verse 10, what is the love of money?

    d. What has happened to some who have longed for it?

3. Look up the word "erred" in the *Strong's* and tell what you learn about it.

4. Describe how you could be affected if you are not careful.

5. According to I Timothy 6:11, how should the Christian handle the desire for money?

1. Write out Luke 14:33.

2. Prayerfully write out the following verses in Luke 12.

   a. Verse 29:

   b. Verse 30:

   c. Verse 31:

   d. Verse 32:

   e. Verse 33:

   f. Verse 34:

3. How do you explain these verses in view of our American lifestyle of hoarding possessions and striving "to get ahead." Would you say that just because "everybody does it" means that it is alright to disobey the Lord's words?

4. Pray-read the story told in Mark 10:17-22 five times. Search your heart honestly before God and ask Him to show you the hold riches still have on you. Explain how you have been affected.

Look up the following verses and tell what you learn about giving.

1. Leviticus 25:35

2. Deuteronomy 15:7

3. Proverbs 11:24

4. Proverbs 21:13

5. Ecclesiastes 5:10, 13

6. Ezekiel 33:31

7. Malachi 3:8

8. Matthew 6:1

9. Luke 12:15

American Christians have allowed themselves to be convinced that they *must* sustain the rich lifestyle that they have been accustomed to in the past. Their greed has caused them to miss one of the richest blessings God has to offer His people: living without all of the entanglements of the world.

Just like it really is possible to have a rich and fulfilling life without television, so it is possible to live without microwaves, stereos, new cars, nice houses and all of the other *things* that we allow to *possess us*.

There is a wonderful freedom and liberty in not owning things. You don't have to worry about a fire destroying all that you own! You don't have to worry about someone ripping you off! You don't have to worry about getting the money together to buy other nice things to keep up "the look."

There is a wonderful sense of contentment that comes with living a simple lifestyle.

1. Prayerfully write out I Timothy 6:6-8.

2. Prayerfully write out Matthew 6:19-21.

3. Prayerfully write out Luke 9:23-25.

4. Explain what God has shown you this week about possessions and write out any new commitments you feel you are ready to make. **Don't make a commitment to God that you will forsake later.**

In January 1956, the most publicized missionary massacre of the twentieth century occurred in the jungles of Ecuador. Jim Elliot, a graduate of Wheaton College and four other young missionaries were ambushed and killed by the Auca Indians they were trying to bring the Gospel to. While still in college Elliot had written, "He is no fool who gives what he cannot keep to gain what he cannot lose."

None of the missionaries had come to Ecuador to minister to the Auca tribe. While there ministering to other tribes, they began hearing stories of a fierce tribe of Indians who murdered any white man who stumbled into their territory. As the five missionaries would often meet and discuss various things of mutual interest, the idea of reaching out to the Aucas began to gradually intrigue them more and more. As they continued to seek God on the idea, it became evident to all that God wanted them to push forward with the project. Knowing full well the danger, Jim Elliot told his wife Elizabeth, "If that's the way God wants it to be, I'm ready to die for the salvation of the Aucas." Undaunted, they carefully laid out a game plan to share the Gospel with the Indians.

The first step in the project was for Nate Saint to fly over the Auca territory until discovering one of their villages. After several days of flying, Nate spotted a large thatch house in a clearing. The next step was to try to establish communication with the people. Nate had devised a way to let things down to the ground by rope, by flying in tight circles high up in the air. By this method, he was able to give them machetes, flashlights and other presents in an attempt to win their friendship.

For the next several months, the missionaries continued to drop gifts to the Aucas. They would also fly low and, speaking over a loudspeaker in the Auca tongue say, "We like you! We like you! We have come to visit you." The people began looking forward to their visits and were soon smiling and waving at the missionaries in the strange flying machine. Then the Indians actually began sending their own gifts back up in the bucket that was lowered down to them. One time it was a squirrel, another time a parrot.

The missionaries finally felt that the time was right for them to see the Aucas in person. They found a sand bar on the Curaray River that Nate felt he could land safely on and the little crew picked the date of January 3. That morning Nate flew the other four into the spot they had christened "Palm Beach," and made another trip over to the Auca village. "Come tomorrow to the river!" he called out over the loudspeaker. Nothing happened until three days later when three Aucas suddenly appeared on the far bank of the river: two girls and a young man. The missionaries tried to speak to them as well as they could, in the few phrases they had managed to pick up. The Indians jabbered away. The man kept touching the Cessna so Nate opened the door and coaxed him to get in. Incredibly, Nate was able to take the young Indian on a flight over his own village. The man laughed and shouted with glee.

They stayed for some time and finally departed. The missionaries were ecstatic over their unexpected success. The next day, no Indians came to visit. Nate went up in the plane the following day and spotted a group of men walking toward the camp. He radioed his wife of the good news, "A commission of ten is coming. Pray for us. This is the day!" He set the next scheduled transmission at 4:30 p.m. and signed off.

At 4:30, Nate's wife turned on the radio and tried to reach her husband. She didn't receive a response. That night all five of the wives tossed and turned in worried sleep. The next day another missionary pilot flew over the area. He radioed back that the plane had been stripped of its fabric and the men were nowhere to be seen. Something was wrong.

The following day a search party was issued. The men were discovered speared to death. While burying the bodies, a *Life* magazine photographer arrived. The story he told made it the missionary story of the century. It touched multitudes of people, with many offering their lives in service to reach the Aucas. Incredibly, through a series of miraculous events, one month after the massacre, two of the wives were able to bring Christ to the killers of their husbands. Every one of the killers came to Christ, with one later becoming a martyr himself as he attempted to bring the gospel to another tribe of Aucas.

WEEK 23: REAL FAITH

Monday   BY FAITH YOU ARE SAVED

MEMORY VERSE: I JOHN 5:3-4

Look up the following verses and tell what you learn about faith.

1. Habakkuk 2:4

2. John 3:15-16, 36

3. Romans 5:1

4. Romans 10:9, 17

5. Ephesians 2:8-9

6. Hebrews 11:1, 6

7. James 1:5-6

There are two kinds of faith: temporal and eternal. There *are* those who believe there is a God. They *do* believe that one day they will stand before Him. They *do* believe that Jesus Christ died and rose from the dead. But it is a *temporal faith* that is based in this world (it is not born out of *true repentance*). When a person truly repents of his sins, he gives his life to God.

1. Look up the word "belief" in the *Vine's* and describe what it really means.

2. Look up the words "reliance" and "credence" in an English dictionary and explain what the difference is between the two.

3. Look up James 2:13-26 and answer the following questions.

    a. Read verses 13-17 and explain what you think James was referring to when he spoke of "works."

    b. Read verses 18-20 and explain what it means to you to believe.

4. Read Matthew 7:21-23. Explain why you think the works mentioned are *not* the works of an *"eternal faith."*

1. Christians often forget where their home is. Write out Philippians 3:20.

2. The Bible teaches that we are citizens of heaven, living temporarily behind "enemy lines" as soldiers of Christ. A.W. Tozer said the following:

   "In the early days, when Christianity exercised a dominant influence over American thinking, men conceived the world to be a battleground. Our fathers believed in sin and the devil and hell as constituting one force; and they believed in God and righteousness and heaven as the other. These were opposed to each other in the nature of them forever in deep, grave, irreconcilable hostility. Man, so our fathers held, had to choose sides; he could not be neutral. For him it must be life or death, heaven or hell; and if he chose to come out on God's side, he could expect open war with God's enemies. The fight would be real and deadly and would last as long as life continued here below. Men looked forward to heaven as a return from the wars, a laying down of the sword to enjoy in peace the home prepared for them....

   "How different today: the fact remains the same but the interpretation has changed completely. Men think of the world not as a *battleground* but as a *playground*. We are not here to fight, we are here to frolic. We are not in a foreign land, we are at home."[34]

   In view of Tozer's remarks, write out meditatively each of the following verses.

   a. II Timothy 2:3-4

   b. I Peter 2:11

3. Expressing an "eternal faith" really means nothing more than having an abiding consciousness of eternity, and living one's daily life with it in mind. If you *knew* this was the last day of your life, and that in a few hours you would be standing before God, how would you act? What would you do with your time? How would you respond to people's unkindness?

   a. Write out a description of what that day would be like for you.

   b. Explain what is stopping you from living that way *every* day.

1. Quickly read over the entire eleventh chapter of Hebrews. Having considered all of the stories outlined in this great chapter about faith, what one thing (besides faith) stood out about the lives of these people?

2. Did you see that each person described lived life in obedience to the will of God? This is the real testing ground of faith—living one's life in obedience to God's will, whatever that may be. Write out Matthew 7:21.

3. Going back to Hebrews 11, can you see that the more a person must be in a position to *trust* God, the more faith he is exhibiting?

   The following is a list of opposite scenarios. Look at each one, think about which would require more faith in God, and circle either "a" or "b".

   a. Living a middle-class, suburban life, and going to church, or
   b. moving into a ghetto to work with drug addicts

   a. Living in the United States, or
   b. living in some other country to share the gospel.

   a. Sitting in church being fed on Wednesday night, or
   b. gathering food and clothes and taking them down to the homeless shelter.

   a. Living life with good health, or
   b. living faithfully to God even though you are paralyzed.

   a. Living with all of life's conveniences and gadgets, or
   b. living on the bare minimum and giving the rest to missions.

   a. Preaching to thousands in an auditorium on a regular basis, or
   b. quietly living out your faith before Indians in the jungles of the Amazon.

   a. Having a "successful" Christian radio show, or
   b. being a meek servant who never seeks or receives recognition.

   a. Being in demand as an evangelist all over the country, or
   b. being tortured for your faith in some Communist prison cell.

Dear brothers and sisters, it is not that being an American Christian is a crime, or that being "successful" in ministry in this country is somehow automatically wrong. It's just that we in America so often bring a worldly (American) concept of success into God's kingdom. The real heroes of the faith aren't the big names (although some *are* dear men of godly faith). The real heroes are those who quietly live out a true, Christian faith of selflessly putting others before themselves. To express real faith in God simply means that you have such a deep sense of belief in Him, that you are willing to go through anything while on this earth to please Him and stay in His will.

4. Write any new views you might have about what real "faith" is.

To be "faithful" means nothing more than to act as one would act who is full of faith. To be full of faith about something means to act as though you really believe it! Let me give an illustration. If I go to work for a company, I am putting my faith in the boss of that company, that at the end of my first week, he will give me a paycheck for my efforts. Every day I work there, I continue to put my confidence in him. I place my confidence in this man's integrity that he is going to do what he has agreed to do. As an outgrowth of that faith, I show up for work everyday, doing what *I* am supposed to do. In other words, I am faith*ful*.

1. Look up the word "faith" in the *Strong's* dictionary. Tell what you learn.

2. Now look up the word "faithful" in the *Strong's* dictionary and tell what you learn about it.

3. Did you notice the number of the Greek word that both of these words are derivatives of (3982)? Look that word up and tell what you learn.

4. Read the parable Jesus gave in Matthew 25:14-30 and answer the following questions. (I know you already know it, but read it carefully again.)

   a. What did the master call the first two servants?

   b. What did he promise them?

   c. According to verse 30, what did he call the third servant?

   d. Write out James 2:20.

   e. Looking at verse 29, what is Jesus talking about? Explain your answer.

In 1965, the Christian western world was stunned with the story of a simple, Lutheran pastor from behind the Iron Curtain. He had been released by the government of Rumania to the Hebrew Christian Alliance for the price of $10,000. What he brought out of that closed country was a stunning and tragic story of severe persecution of Christians by the Communist government. Pastor Wurmbrand testified to a Senate subcommittee what was happening to Christians behind the Iron Curtain. He stripped to the waist, showing deep scars inflicted over the fourteen years he spent in various prisons.

Although raised an avowed atheist, Richard accepted Christ as a young man. In 1945, the Communists seized Rumania, and began a crackdown on all churches in the country. For the next three years, Richard and his wife Sabine secretly began ministering to the people of his area and also to the Russian soldiers who were so prevalent in Rumania in the forties.

In 1948, Richard and Sabine were both arrested. Sabine served three years as a slave-laborer, leaving their nine-year-old son to fend for himself. Two Christian ladies attempted to help him. For this kindness they were arrested and beaten so badly that one remained crippled for the rest of her life. Another lady tried to take care of him and was arrested and sentenced to eight years in prison for helping the family of a prisoner. In the process of her arrest, her bones were broken and all her teeth kicked out.

It would be eight long years before Richard would see "freedom" again. His wife was told that he had died in prison, and she existed this whole time thinking he was dead. His sufferings were horrible. He tells of being hung upside down on ropes and beaten so hard that his body swung back and forth. Sometimes they would put him in a large ice-box until the point that he was ready to freeze to death. Then they would pull him out, warm him up and do it again—over and over again. Other times he would be put in a wooden box just slightly bigger than he, with dozens of sharp nails driven into every side. He would be left in there for hours upon hours. If he remained absolutely straight, he would be O.K. But if he re-laxed even a little, the nails would pierce his flesh.

Wurmbrand tells the story of a pastor named Florescu who was tortured with red-hot iron pokers and knives. After being beaten senseless, starving rats were driven into his cell through a pipe in the wall. He could not sleep or relax as the rats would attack him as soon as he let down his guard. He was forced to stand like this for two weeks, day and night. When he still refused to betray his brethren, they brought in his fourteen-year-old son. They began to whip the boy in front of this dear pastor until he was half mad. Finally he yelled out to his son that he must comply with them. His son answered him, "Father, don't do me the injustice to have a traitor as a parent." Enraged, the torturers beat the young boy to death, splattering blood all over the cell in the process. The pastor was never the same again.

Wurmbrand also tells of another time that Christians were tied to crosses for four days and nights. The crosses were put on the floor and hundreds of other prisoners had to fulfill their bodily functions over the faces and bodies of the Christians. Then the crosses were erected again while the Communists mocked and jeered their "savior."

After eight and a half years of such treatment, Wurmbrand was finally released. Upon being released, he went right to work ministering again to the underground church in Rumania. For over three years he ministered in this fashion, until again, he was arrested. This time he spent five and a half years in prison.

It was strictly forbidden to preach to other prisoners, and if caught, the preacher would be unmercifully beaten. Richard and several other prisoners struck up a deal of sorts with their torturers: they would preach and the Communists would beat them! He tells of the time one prisoner was caught in the middle of a message, taken out and beaten to a pulp and thrown back into the cell. He picked himself up again and said, "Now, brethren, where did I leave off when I was interrupted?"

Richard Wurmbrand and countless others have withstood unspeakable tortures for their faith in Christ. Their rewards will be great in heaven for what they have endured!

WEEK 24: ON YOUR OWN!

Monday

MEMORY VERSE: YOU PICK YOUR OWN!

It's time to prepare for life after *The Walk Of Repentance*. Each day this week, pick a subject you want to study in the Bible, and list verses and what they mean to you.

1. What is the subject/word you have chosen to study today?

2. Look up the word you are studying today in the *Strong's* or *Vine's* and tell what you learn about it.

3. Pick out six to eight verses about the subject and tell what you learn about it

    1.

    2.

    3.

    4.

    5.

    6.

Tuesday

1. What is the subject/word you have chosen to study today?

2. Look up today's word you are studying in *Strong's* or *Vine's* and tell what you learn about it.

3. Pick out six to eight verses about the subject and tell what you learn about it.

   1.

   2.

   3.

   4.

   5.

   6.

   7.

Wednesday

1. What is the subject/word you have chosen to study today?

2. Look up today's word you are studying in *Strong's* or *Vine's* and tell what you learn about it.

3. Pick out six to eight verses about the subject and tell what you learn about it.

   1.

   2.

   3.

   4.

   5.

   6.

   7.

Thursday

1. What is the subject/word you have chosen to study today?

2. Look up today's word you are studying in *Strong's* or *Vine's* and tell what you learn about it.

3. Pick out six to eight verses about the subject and tell what you learn about it.

    1.

    2.

    3.

    4.

    5.

    6.

    7.

Friday

1. What is the subject/word you have chosen to study today?

2. Look up today's word you are studying in *Strong's* or *Vine's* and tell what you learn about it.

3. Pick out six to eight verses about the subject and tell what you learn about it.

    1.

    2.

    3.

    4.

    5.

    6.

    7.

Take a moment, in this your last study, and reflect on some of the stories you have read. Do you see the common thread throughout these stories, of people who were willing to suffer if need be to bring Christ to the lost? Suffering has been a hallmark of the true Christian faith from the beginning. Paul said in II Timothy 3:12, "And indeed, *all* who desire to live godly in Christ Jesus will be persecuted." It is as simple as the law of gravity: if you desire to live a godly life, you *will* be persecuted. The truth of the matter is that we in America have become so acclimated to a sterile and pain-free lifestyle of comfort, that we simply are not willing to suffer for Christ.

But the suffering wasn't the issue with these dear saints. They were willing to suffer, but why? The answer is that they had come to know Christ in a wonderful way. Once they had come truly to know Him, they were willing to endure *anything* to be able to share that joy with others.

We in America have kept ourselves insulated from God with the things of this world. We have so filled our lives with worldliness that we have no room for God, thus we never really get to know Him, and thus we have nothing to share with others but our own dogmatic viewpoints.

Christianity down through the centuries has always simply meant pouring one's life out to others. Christianity in America now has become more of a matter of head knowledge, "ministers" competing with each other over who has the biggest church, the most radio stations, the biggest following. The speaker who can best appeal to the intellect or emotions of the people will be the one with the largest following. We have missed the whole concept of what Christianity is: selflessly living lives of mercy toward those around us. James said, "This is pure and undefiled religion in the sight of our God and Father, to visit orphans and widows in their distress, and to keep oneself unstained by the world." (James 1:27).

Jesus said, "A new commandment I give to you, that you love one another; even as I have loved you, that you also love one another. By this all men will know that you are My disciples, if you have love for one another." (John 13:34-35). This commandment is every bit as real as the commandment not to commit fornication, and yet we lift up high one commandment in the Church and totally disregard the other! Do we *really* love others? People often think that because they don't hurt others, they love others. That's not love! Love means you are willing to sacrifice for others, to put the needs of others before your own.

Jesus said that the world would know us by one thing: our love for one another. But how difficult it is to find volunteers to go to the nursing home, to feed the poor—or even to work for Pure Life Ministries. People have their own agenda—*their* will for their lives.

The stories you have read over the last six months have been stories of those who had really experienced the love of Jesus Christ and sought to pour out that love to others. As you finish this curriculum, what will happen with your life? Will it change? Or will you just be one more comfortable, self-centered, American "Christian?"

Perhaps you are thinking that you *really would* like to go deeper in this Christian walk. What should you do? How do you know God's will for your life?

God's will for your life is *love and mercy for others.* Just find a place you can start pouring your life into others—and not in some way that's going to bring attention to yourself. Go to the local convalescent hospital and start visiting people there, sharing Jesus if you have the opportunity. Find a jail ministry and get involved; they always need volunteers. Go to the local soup kitchen and offer to help them on Saturdays. Go to your pastor and tell him that you would like to volunteer quietly to do the job around the church that nobody else is willing to do.

Just start *doing something.* As you do, I assure you that God will sit up and take notice! If you show Him a heart of mercy for others, He will then give you more clear direction on what He wants for your life. But He won't (can't) speak to you if you are spending your life in front of a television, and selfishly thinking only of yourself.

Share the mercy and love with others that God has shared with you. "Freely you have received, now freely give!" Who knows, maybe someday people will be writing books about *your* life of mercy!

BIBLIOGRAPHY

1. Richard Wurmbrand, *If Prison Walls Could Speak*, Christian Missions to the Communist World, Middlebury, IN, 1972, p.78

2. Eberhard Arnold, *the Early Christians*, Plough Publishing, Rifton, NY, 1979, p.80-81

3. W. Grinton Berry, *Foxe's Book of Martyrs*, Baker Book House, Grand Rapids, MI, 1978, p.28

4. James Gilchrist Lawson, *Deeper Experiences of Famous Christians*, The Warner Press, Anderson, IN, 1911, p.81

5. *ibid*, p.82

6. Basil Miller, *William Carey The Father of Modern Missions*, Bethany House Publishers, Minneapolis, MN, 1952, p.54

7. *ibid*, p.105-106

8. *ibid*, p.149

9. Watchman Nee, *Spiritual Authority*, Christian Fellowship Publishers, New York, NY, 1972, p.118

10. Faith Coxe Bailey, *Adoniram Judson America's First Foreign Missionary*, Moody Press, Chicago, 1955, p.70

11. W.E. Vine, *Vine's Expository Dictionary*, Fleming H. Revell Co., Old Tappan, NJ, 1981, p.290

12. Mrs. J.H. Worcester, Jr. *David Livingstone First To Cross Africa With The Gospel*, Moody Press, Chicago, 1989, p.19

13. *ibid*, p.32

14. *ibid*, p.66-67

15. *ibid*, p.89

16. J. Hudson Taylor, *Hudson Taylor*, Bethany House Publishers, Minneapolis, MN, 1987, p.21

17. *ibid*, p.68-69

18. *ibid*, p.145

19. Rosalind Goforth, *Jonothan Goforth*, Bethany House Publishers, Minneapolis, MN, 1937, p.45

20. *ibid*, p.48

21. *ibid*, p.82

22. James & Marti Hefley, *By Their Blood*, Baker Book House, Grand Rapids, MI, 1979, p.18-19

23. *ibid*, p.19-20

24. *ibid*, p.21

25. *ibid*.

26. *ibid*, p.20

27. *ibid*, p.56

28. *ibid*, p.58-59

29. *ibid*.

30. *ibid*, p.339-340

31. *ibid*, p.482-483

32. Corrie Ten Boom, *The Hiding Place*, Bantam Books, New York, NY, 1971, p.194-195

33. Deitrich Bonhoeffer, *The Cost of Discipleship*, Collier Books, New York, NY, 1937, p.47-48

34. Warren W. Wiersbe, *The Best of A.W. Tozer*, Baker Book House, Grand Rapids, MI, 1978, p.84-85

A LAMP UNTO MY FEET

A 12-WEEK STUDY THROUGH PSALM 119

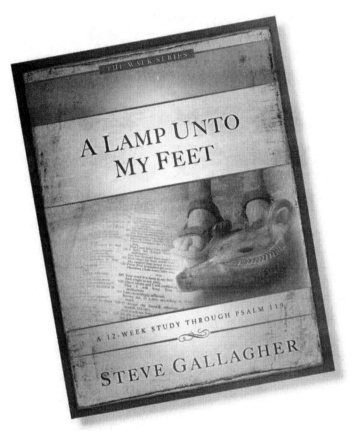

EVERY READER WILL BE BROUGHT INTO A DEEPER LOVE, RESPECT AND APPRECIATION FOR GOD'S WORD.

Every true believer is daily moving toward his eternal destination. However, before that final crossing into the land of immortality, the Christian pilgrim must first travel through a hostile empire, fraught with "dangers, toils and snares." How will he find his way through this land of shadows? Fortunately, the "Father of lights" has not left us to fend for ourselves; but rather, He has provided a roadmap, the Word of God. Little wonder that David christened it *A Lamp Unto My Feet*.

A sequel to Gallagher's *The Walk of Repentance*, this is a 12-week journey through the beautiful Psalm 119. This practical, personal study is a great resource for any individual seeking guidance in the midst of life's struggles. Through daily meditation readings and questions for reflection, believers will be asked to consider the truths of Scripture. At each week's end, they will also read about the life of David, a man after God's own heart and author of this epic psalm. Every reader will be brought into a deeper love, respect and appreciation for God's Word.

PRESSING ON TOWARD THE HEAVENLY CALLING

A 12-WEEK STUDY THROUGH THE PRISON EPISTLES

THIS TWELVE-WEEK STUDY OF EPHESIANS, PHILIPPIANS AND COLOSSIANS WILL INSPIRE EVERY BELIEVER TO KEEP "PRESSING ON."

The Prison Epistles are a menagerie of profound revelations about the kingdom of God, accumulated by a man who for many years enjoyed unbroken fellowship with the Lord. Each epistle possesses its own unique style and theme, but in this study they join together as a "fountain of life" to those who love God.

Paul wrote these three books toward the end of his life. Having "fought the good fight…finished the course…kept the faith," he was now moving toward "the crown of righteousness, which the Lord, the righteous Judge" would award him. (II Timothy 4:6-8) For nearly thirty years, the "apostle to the Gentiles" had been pouring out his life and pointing multitudes to Christ. Now, his life and his letters come alive in a practical and personal way. Through this twelve-week study, every believer will be inspired to join Paul's quest in *Pressing On Toward the Heavenly Calling*.